To Elizabeth 9/30/22

Love,
Janice Hope

JANICE HOPE

Love Never Dies

Spiritual Insights About Suicide, Life and Love From Kevin in Heaven

Are you here Kev?

Yep! Always there for U Mom!

Love You as BIG as the Expanding Universe!

FORWARD BY CHRISTIAN SØRENSEN, SPIRITUAL LEADER, SEASIDE CENTER FOR SPIRITUAL LIVING

Praise for *Love Never Dies*

*"**Love Never Dies** is a unique and vulnerable tribute to the never-ending love between a mother and son. Janice Hope's mystical journey through grief as she reconstructs her life after Kevin's sudden death, inspires us all to reach beyond our limited reality; To open our hearts and minds to the true potential that it is possible to remain connected to our loved ones after they transition from this world."*

—**Kalli Holmes Sørensen**, a midwife of feminine consciousness and a visionary leader in women's empowerment for over three decades

*"**Love Never Dies** is a Spiritual gold mine for those who seek solace over the loss of their child or loved one, especially when suicide was chosen to escape the torment from their pain and suffering. Janice is a living example of the power of Love and what it means to "knock, and the door shall be opened."*

—**Woody Fulmor,** Advanced Practitioner of Structural Integration for over 40 years

"I have been impacted by the death and suicide of friends and family members. It's not easy for a teenager to push aside grief and hard events. However, I now see that it's never too late to work through such feelings. This book inspired me to try to reconnect with a close friend who has recently died, using objects I have kept to remember her.

As I pursue a career in a medical field full of tragedy, **Love Never Dies** *has reminded me that through my past, present, and future, regardless of beliefs or ideals, I can find a reason for everything. With time and love, it's possible to find healing and peace in each soul."*

—**Gabriel Lopez**, 18, Emergency Medical Technician (EMT) Student

"Losing a son to suicide must be one of the hardest tragedies to endure for a mother. What good can come from such a horrific event? Janice Hope is such a mother, and she has turned this deep loss into triumph. Having been intuitive since she was very young, she knew that contact with the Spirit world is possible. When her beloved Kevin took his own life, Janice was determined to connect with him.

Not only did communication happen, but she also learned so much through ongoing discussions with Kevin. The result of her journey is astounding, even to the biggest skeptic. In genuine, heartfelt words Janice shares what she discovered from the 'other side' to provide healing and help people.

The love between mother and son is tangible, and it continues beyond the veil that separates the worlds here and there. This is a must-read for anyone dealing with the ensuing grief of losing of a loved one or those overwhelmed by life's challenges.

The message Janice conveys is deeply comforting. Her book will also be an eye-opener for those who still doubt that contact with the 'other side' is not only possible, but meaningful and insightful. It offers healing to the living, and perhaps to those on the Spirit world as well.

I highly recommend this fascinating read!"

—**Rev. Uki MacIsaac**, Spiritual Intuitive, UkiMacIsaac.com

"I was honored to help Janice with her endeavor to share an experience that causes the deepest agony imaginable for a mother. Her vulnerability in expressing love and anger from her pain is admirable. These examples kept reminding me that forgiveness, honesty, and willingness to feel through an emotion will bring miracles of healing. I could only hope to have such courage. Janice set a course to help us understand that **Love Never Dies.** *"*

— **Kathann**

"Janice Hope shares a timeless message that forgiveness is the pathway to peace, never-ending love, healing, and self-awareness.

The suicide of her son was the ultimate test in trusting higher powers to guide her through the worst nightmare that any parent can live with. Through many stories and events, we come to learn how this love and willingness to understand and forgive binds them and all of us together for eternity. This is the Divine Plan.

The breath work which Janice uses is a tool constantly available to everyone, anywhere and anytime. Her stories demonstrate how this practice never fails to bring relief and it supports a quiet healing space in the mind, heart, body, and spirit.

I found so many wonderful and insightful takeaways. I especially encourage you to read it to discover Kevin's insights about 'The God Glue' and 'The God Vibe.' She provides resources and information reminding us that NO ONE has to suffer alone."

—**Brenda Gunn**

"This is your go-to book for understanding that **Love Never Dies** *between you and your loved ones!*

Janice Hope writes so beautifully, powerfully and authentically about her son Kevin's life with such depth and intimacy.

I couldn't put it down! I kept a pen nearby to underline many insightful messages.

I highly recommend this book! A classic, for all of us— young and not so young, to know there is always, help! And that we are also loved beyond measure.

A must read!"

—**Melanie Lococo**, M.S., former Director of Giving at Hay House, Author & Transformational Coach, MelanieLococo.com

"To the unconsolable... have faith. This remarkable story engenders hope and healing for those left behind. Between mother and son, Janice and Kevin show us without any doubt that our connection with our loved ones never ends. Now that Kevin is in heaven, he has gone on to evolve and expand in profound ways. A mother's sorrow is forever, but the 'sting' can fade through forgiveness and understanding."

—Hollis Fulmor

"I was greatly moved, even to tears, by the timeless and healing message of **Love Never Dies**. *I felt so close to Kevin and his mother, Janice. Every word, from beginning to end, served as a 'sacred salve' for my grieving soul. A missing link in the chain of love; utterly transformational. As I read, my heart opened and was soothed of the pain I have endured for way too long. Tears no longer robbed me of my joy, but suddenly cleansed me to live fully again. Now that I understand the true nature of life and death, I stand in the light of compassion for everyone and that, gratefully, includes myself.*

Thank you, dear Janice for having 'ears that hear,' and for passing this Heavenly auria along to those of us seeking solace, for indeed, I now see that Love Never Dies."

—Carolynsue Dickens

LOVE NEVER DIES

Spiritual Insights About Suicide, Life and Love from Kevin in Heaven

Janice Hope

GLOBAL WELLNESS MEDIA
STRATEGIC EDGE INNOVATIONS PUBLISHING
LOS ANGELES, TORONTO, MONTREAL

Copyright © 2022 by **Janice Hope**. All rights reserved.

No part of this publication may be reproduced, distributed, or transmitted in any form or by any means, including photocopying, recording, or other electronic or mechanical methods, without the prior written permission of the author, except in the case of brief quotations embodied in critical reviews and certain other non-commercial uses permitted by copyright law.

For permission requests, send an email to book@janicehope.com

First Edition. Published by:
Global Wellness Media
Strategic Edge Innovations Publishing
340 S Lemon Ave #2027
Walnut, California 91789-2706
(866) 467-9090
StrategicEdgeInnovations.com

Publisher's Note: The views expressed in this work are solely those of the authors and do not necessarily reflect the views of the publisher, and the publisher hereby disclaims any responsibilities for them.

Cover design: Eric D. Groleau
Book design: Global Wellness Media

Love Never Dies / Janice Hope. —1st ed.
ISBN: 978-1-957343-16-7 (Paperback)
ISBN: 978-1-957343-17-4 (ePub)

Disclaimer

The information contained herein is not intended to be a substitute for professional evaluation and therapy with a health professional. If you are experiencing any health issues, you need to seek professional help.

This book is based on the author's personal experience and other real-life examples. To protect privacy, names have been changed in some cases.

Table of Contents

Foreword xv
Acknowledgements xxi
Additional Materials & Resources xxv

Introduction 1
Chapter 1: Hearing and Seeing from Beyond 3
Chapter 2: Journey to the Dump Truck 11
Chapter 3: Kevin's Passing 23
Chapter 4: Our Communication Continues 39
Chapter 5: The God Vibe 49
Chapter 6: A Life Shortened 67
Chapter 7: Awakening Here or There 75
Chapter 8: Don't Give Up 83
Chapter 9: Do Good in the World 91
Chapter 10: The Santa Claus Gift 101
Chapter 11: Clever Boy 111
Chapter 12: In Letting Go Your Heart Expands 117
Chapter 13: The Illusion of Separation 125
Chapter 14: Being in the Flow 131
Chapter 15: Opening to Feelings 143
Chapter 16: Expanded Frequencies 149
Chapter 17: The Other Side 163
Chapter 18: Unconscious Decisions 167
Chapter 19: The Continuum of Love 175

Thankful (by Rebecca Jade) 179
Suggested Resources 181
About the Author 187

Foreword

If you have ever wondered if loved ones can communicate from another dimension after they have passed on from this world, Janice Hope eliminates that doubt. Janice captured a dialogue with her youngest son Kevin who left this world sooner than any mom would want. No mother should have to bury a child. It is just not the natural order of things. Yet for Janice, this heartbreaking moment did come to her life. *Love Never Dies* is her journey to healing through dialoguing with her son. Kevin in heaven assures her that he is not dead, just out of his earth body.

Janice's engaging story begins as a small child alone and lost in the forbidden Black Forest of Germany when she was about to be attacked by a hideous looking, tusk baring, wild boar. When she cries out for help, two angels appeared and transformed a terrorizing moment into one of beauty. Young Janice was led out of the Black Forest by two radiant beings at her sides, back to her home on the edge of the forest. From that moment on, Janice knew she had the ability to see, hear and communicate with beings of another frequency that others could not see.

We travel with Janice from her modeling days to her first relationships and the birth of her boys. She eventually realized that she was continuously giving her power away to her husbands. This led her to discover that her soul's lesson from the classroom of relationships is that she is the one who must change, not her husbands. The ultimate moment of love for her boys came when they wanted to go live with their dad. Yet, somehow, this heartbreaking moment pulled her into a higher vibration than her sadness. In an unexpected twist of awareness, she found herself face to face with Archangel Michael. This Divine Messenger brought the comfort she needed to guide her through this rough time of disbelief.

Janice's intuitive communication developed through soul lessons on this journey through life. This groundwork helped to prepare her for the unfathomable agony of when her almost 25-year-old son, Kevin, took his life. This profound aching led her to explore the depths of her life's disruption. This upheaval revealed that her communication link with Kevin was closer and more direct than a phone call. It was now soul-to-soul communication. Janice came to experience that love really does transcend time and space. The unconditional love that brought them together here is what keeps them connected here after. It is clear that Kevin is not dead; he has just left his earth body behind. His earth suit was no longer needed in his new dimensional playground. Yet the spirit that is Kevin and animated this physical body, putting the twinkle in his eyes, is still alive and active, expressing through his heavenly body. As Paul wrote in 1 Corinthian 15:40, there are bodies celestial and bodies terrestrial.

Kevin in Heaven, who can now find himself in many places at once, helps his mom from the other side find clarity around his suicide. Janice's transcendent love assists her son with his soul's lesson of not needing to run any longer. Janice beautifully captured their dialogue and the details that helped them both navigate through forgiveness, understanding and ultimately, release.

Janice learns that one of the keys for this multidimensional interaction is to remain open and not to become blocked by emotional pain; otherwise, she finds herself going down a dark rabbit hole. She must learn to consciously choose to feel better in order to actually be available to feeling better. As a massage therapist, she learned how the body holds onto pain at the cellular level. She has spent years assisting people in melting the physical tension retained in the body. Janice knows she must go through the pain rather than pushing it down and burying it away. Kevin in Heaven guides mom in allowing what he calls the "God Vibe" to fill the new available space of her soul.

Her first Christmas without her youngest son will open your heart as his Christmas Day visit is a message of love. His synchronistic signs will inspire you to reach out to your loved one on the other side. Janice also shares the soul-warming story of support for her girlfriend who chose to be among the first in California to participate in the "Death

FOREWORD

With Dignity Act." As her dear friend's soul left her physical realm, what she said will leave you with a sense that all is great on the other side.

Janice will help you move into a deeper sense of confidence and trust that there is so much more beyond what is seen. The "God Glue" holds it all together and death is just a perceptual illusion.

This is an open-heart invitation to join her on this journey into an ever-expanding consciousness of love. You will come to know how this love keeps you connected to your beloved who are on the other side of the veil, whether you know it or not. It is your choice whether you want to become conscious of that multidimensional connection. With this book, Janice Hope helps you to link up if you chose this path.

Christian Sørensen
Spiritual Leader,
Seaside Center for Spiritual Living
Author, *Living from the Mountaintop: Be the Mystic You Were Born to Be*

Dedicated to
My Three Sons

MAY WE ALWAYS WALK THE PATH OF LOVE TOGETHER!

Top: Chad, Bottom: Kevin and Arie

Acknowledgements

Three days after my son's memorial, I lay bedridden following a major ankle and foot surgery. My dear friend Kathann, who was then a neighbor, would come and sit with me next to my bed. She was the perfect support as she encouraged me to feel the depth of my loss for Kevin. There was nowhere to run. It was a hard, but perfect setup to begin my healing.

As I shared the amazing connection I had with Kevin, three days after he took his own life, Kathann surprised me. As a clairvoyant and clairaudient, she could not only hear but see Kevin lying next to me. I then realized that she was not just a friend, but a great teacher. She also told me, during one of her loving visits, that someday Kevin and I would be writing a book together and offered to be our editor. I did not have that vision, at that time, and it seemed a bit far-fetched.

After four years and many communications with Kevin, it was clear that my son wanted me to share our conversations with the world. He was hoping that it would bring insight and upliftment to whomever was open to receive. His intention was to prevent anyone from ending their own life.

Kathann had then moved to Minnesota and to my amazement, she still said YES to help with the book after all this time. I am a storyteller, and by no means an accomplished writer. My sentences would run on, and punctuation consisted of way too many exclamation marks! She spent many hours, over a two-year span, sifting through words and making sure it was clearly reflecting the truth of our communications.

Thank you Kathann for your timeless dedication. I have been blessed beyond measure to have such an amazing Guide who is much more than an editor, but a lifelong friend and teacher. You have been a priceless gift truly sent by the Angels. Kevin thanks you as well.

Bringing this book to the light of day, has involved another great soul, my publisher, Eric D. Groleau. Working enthusiastically for months over Zoom, from Toronto, Canada, he believed in the potential and importance of the message. He followed me from Baja, Guatemala, and back to Encinitas, California, to make my dream a reality. His dedication and insight to having this book be the best it could possibly be, in every way, never ceased to amaze me! His work with words was done with great sensitivity and intuition. I would often comment, "How come I didn't say that in the first place?" Or "Brilliantly done, Eric!" or, "Yes, this feels right." His deep insight into the story also inspired his design for the beautiful cover. I will always love you, your contagious smile, and appreciate having you in my life.

The true Love that has kept me going is my husband, Bryan. When the "Do not Disturb" sign would go up on the door, he knew that I was diving deep inside again. Hours later, dinner would be waiting for me along with a big hug, accompanied by a serenade from his ukulele. The upliftment from his joyful songs, along with his loving smile and energy, encouraged me to sign along! He would always bring me back into the present moment and was the balancing point I needed to get back in the NOW.

When Kevin took his own life, the grief and sadness opened old wounds from our past. Unfortunately, Bryan knew this pain all too well, as he also tragically lost both his brother and his father to suicide within two years of each other.

Bryan's endless support and dedication, along with the depth of his compassion for my feelings, have been a blessing throughout the years.

He spent countless hours honoring my process. His growing patience has been remarkable! I thank you Bryan, for being an amazing co-creator, singing partner and a husband who always looks for the beauty in everything! Thank you for believing in me and encouraging

ACKNOWLEDGEMENTS

me to keep moving forward, no matter what happens. I will Love you always.

I want to thank Reverend Christian Sørensen for his dynamic energy and his deep listening. Every Sunday, he inspires Bryan and I, along with countless others, at Seaside Center for Spiritual Living in Encinitas, California. We appreciate that we can now watch and listen to him as we travel away through live streaming and recorded videos of his talks. They are always uplifting, insightful and encouraging us on our Spiritual path.

I also appreciate his wife, Kalli Sørensen, who brings the feminine heart connection to our community. She has both founded and facilitated many successful women's groups, including Seaside Center for Spiritual Living's Seaside Sisters, a thriving, dynamic community of women. I am honored to be loved and embraced by this dynamic duo who truly live in the Light. Thank You Christian and Kalli.

I want to thank my family, extended family, and friends, who continued to offer their love and support throughout the years. I appreciate your help and interest as I was writing this book. I love you all dearly. The Love from every single one of you makes a difference. You know who you are… I am blessed to have you all in my life!

Additional Materials & Resources

Access your Additional Materials & Resources referenced throughout this book at JaniceHope.com/lovebonus

Thank you for reading our book. We hope it provides valuable insights, understanding and healing. We truly wish you to feel all the Love available in your life!

—Kevin and Janice

Our last picture together in 2015

Introduction

It takes courage for me to write this book and share these most intimate connections with my son Kevin and to be so transparent about my personal and spiritually journey. He has shared so much with me in the last seven years since his passing. I have selected some of the most important or significant ones to demonstrate how loved ones can connect and help us on our physical journey from the other side.

I still find it amazing that I can hear messages from loved ones. I realize this as an opportunity to weave together the physical and spirit worlds. The wisdom carried by our Angels, Guides and Loved Ones is extremely valuable and I wanted to share these jewels in this book.

I now better understand why this happened to Kevin and I am dedicated to reminding people that love and help are always available and waiting. My intention in sharing these important messages is to bring hope, comfort, or an awakening to those in need.

I hope this book will provide peace and comfort by demonstrating that love never dies. It is a vulnerable and loving conversation between my son and me. It includes timeless messages and deep lessons around the challenges in life. This can benefit anyone seeking a deeper understanding about life and empower them with tools and resources.

We all need to remember that we are never alone, and that we are loved unconditionally. It is important to be receptive to Love, and to messages of loving encouragements.

Chapter 1

Hearing and Seeing from Beyond

*"For he shall give his Angels charge
over thee, to keep thee in all ways."*
—Psalm 91:11

Working as a Massage Therapist and Intuitive Healing Facilitator for over thirty-five years, I would always ask clients permission to say a little prayer out loud and call in all the Love and support available for them. In working with hundreds of people throughout the years, not one has ever said no. With the person lying comfortably on the massage table and with my hands cradling their neck I would say, "I now call forth the Golden Light of Love, the Christ Heart Energy, all your Angels, Guides and Loved Ones who wish to be with you today to bring balance to your Body, Mind and Spirit, and I call in all my Angels to help me be a clear channel for this Love and Light for your highest and best good." I would guide my clients to breathe in a certain way to help them to relax into the moment and I would then drop into stillness. I was usually guided to a tightness they held in their body, then my fingers and hands would automatically know what to do and the journey would unfold.

One day, I was working on a client. I'll call him Randy, a fictitious name, for I will never share any of my clients' names.

I could feel Randy's pain just enough to know what needed to be done. I would call it *"issues in the tissues."* This was truly a guided journey, way beyond *a regular massage*. For some, I could sense that's all they wanted or were open to, but for so many I was clear that there was so much more going on. Hands-on healing does not always result in physical healing, it can go beyond to that what is truly needed. Traumas, be they physical, mental or emotional, if not fully released, understood and healed, will be held deep within the body tissues. These, in turn, can cause illness or pain that begs to be discovered and released. I have learned to listen and trust my guidance and feel deeply into the person on the massage table in front of me. The physical and energetic blockages would become clear to me and as I remind them to breathe, the journey would begin. This breathing was especially important in opening to more ease in their body and allowing this session to become transformative. How deep and vast a healing can go becomes truly clear to me as I work on a client.

Randy was a wonderful artist who came to see me as he was trying to find a cure for Hodgkin's lymphoma, which doctors had recently diagnosed in him. He had earnestly been traveling all over the country to find a cure and now he was lying on my table. My prayer was said and almost immediately I felt a male presence on my left side. I took a deep breath, listened, and then said, "Randy, I feel a male presence here with me, a grandfather or father who is here for you."

"I doubt that." Randy replied. "Yes, it feels like your father," I said, "Is he on the other side?" "Yes, I can't imagine him wanting to see me" was his pained response. Ah, I thought, this is going to be a tough one, but the male voice was loud and clear, so I continued. "He wants to say how sorry he is for being so hard on you and how proud he is with your having become such a wonderful artist." "Well, he had a hard time *showing me* that!" Randy harshly replied. "I hear that Randy, but now he's showing me a little worn stuffed teddy bear. Does that mean something to you?" "Oh my God," he exclaimed, "I still have that little teddy bear he gave me sitting in a chair next to my bed." Oh boy, I thought; *now* we have a connection.

"Breathe Randy, breathe," I said, as my hands moved over his heart. "It is OK," I reassured him, "just breathe." He took another deep breath. Tears were now rolling down his cheeks. I continued, "He's now showing me little trains, a lot of little trains… Does that mean something to you?" "Yes, oh my gosh, he set up our entire basement with an elaborate train track for my brother and me when we were young. This really *is* him." I encouraged Randy to breathe deeper into his heart and allow his father's love in more deeply. "I never felt he loved me. He was a football coach, and I was always a disappointment to him. I wasn't into sports like my brother and my father did not understand me or even like me very much for being different."

His father's voice and presence, very clearly, urged me to continue. "Tell him how sorry I am for the lack of support and understanding I gave him." Randy's father wanted him to know, from his heart, how badly he felt and how much he loved him. Now, I was feeling the deep emotion and tears were rolling down my cheeks. Randy seemed to really embrace his dad's thoughts and heartfelt feelings. He had been waiting for those words and this love all his life and now the time was here.

I let the energy use me as a medium or a bridge between the worlds. I remained in awe about what was transpiring before me. A true healing was happening, but in a way Randy certainly had not expected. This was a powerful process of deep love and humility on his father's part, asking for forgiveness from his son. Now, I knew why Randy was guided to come to see me that day. I also felt how deeply embedded this pain this had been for him. The tears of relief and ease he felt in his body were happening because he was able to forgive his father. The last words Randy's father said were, "I love him so much, please let him know that and thank you."

Randy left that day feeling a deep peace from an unexpected healing with his father. I was grateful and humbled to have witnessed such a softening in his heart before he passed about a month later.

I feel blessed to have witnessed so many healings of the Body and Soul while being guided to do this work. Facilitating this heart opening with so many people is a gift I somehow have been given and it never ceased to *amaze me.*

My journey of hearing and seeing what most others could not started when I was very young and has continued throughout my years. I never thought I would be communicating with loved ones on the other side, let alone with my own child. I will share with you my journey and my experience with Angels and explain how this has unfolded in my life and allowed me to communicate with my son Kevin on the other side. The following story is my first connection to this Love.

MEETING MY ANGELS

The year was 1955, less than ten years after World War II. My father was stationed at Ramstein Air Force Base in Germany and our family lived on the edge of the *forbidden* Black Forest. My brother Gordon was eleven and I was only five. Our parents always warned us *never go into the forest!* "You could get lost, hurt, or even killed! There are bombs and grenades left over from the war. The trees are tall and grow so closely together it becomes dark as night, even in the middle of the day. Large wild boars live in that forest and will eat you for their dinner!" We both solemnly promised never to cross the boundary from our safe backyard and go into the scary dark world of the Black Forest.

One beautiful sunny summer day, I was playing in my bedroom with my dolls. Suddenly, I heard the shouting outside my window. "BANG!" the voice shouted. It was my big brother playing war with the boys. Playing dolls was not as exciting as what he was doing. They were having a great time, but I wasn't allowed to play with the big boys, so I became the invisible little sister. I quietly crept down the stairs to the backyard, being careful not to be seen. Mom's wash was blowing in the afternoon breeze, and I hid behind the gently swaying sheets.

"I got you!" My brother's voice shouted. "No, BANG! I got you!" "I got you first! You are dead!" His friend shouted back. "No, I am not, you missed again," my brother insisted, and the battle continued. Suddenly they turned and ran right into the forest, the *Forbidden Forest!* I couldn't believe it, yet I wanted to follow them. I remembered my parent's warnings to *"NEVER GO"* there, but I could not stop myself, I had to follow. It is OK, I thought, my big brother was doing it.

I ran fast, hoping to not lose them, but the boys' voices became faint and further away until I hardly heard them. I could not go fast enough to keep up. It was getting darker as I went deeper in the forest. The trees were so dense, the sun was struggling to reach the forest floor. It was such a *creepy place*. My foot tripped over an old gas mask from the war, and I was scared. *What have I done?* I thought. It was a heart-pounding moment, and I was very afraid. As I went deeper, stumbling to catch up to my brother, I did not want to be the invisible little sister anymore. Suddenly, I just wanted to go home.

The forest wrapped me with its thick musty dampness, and it quickly became black and hard to see. Narrow beams of light, like huge flashlights, penetrated down through the denseness of tall, skinny trees onto the forest floor. I moved between those light beams, trying to find my brother. The sharp cracking sounds of twigs and branches, breaking beneath my feet, echoed through the forest like gunshots!

Suddenly, before me in the next shaft of light, stood a *HUGE* wild boar. It was the ugliest and scariest thing I had ever seen. Deadly large tusks spiked right out of his snout. We both froze, staring into each other's eyes. *I was terrified!*

The boar grunted and snorted. My heart was pounding hard, and my body jerked in fear. *This is the end of me,* I thought. How could I escape? What could I do? I felt helpless, then like magic, I remembered a picture hanging over my bed of a Guardian Angel helping two children cross a rickety bridge. In my head I screamed, *"HELP ME ANGELS, HELP ME!"*

Instantly, a strange yet comforting feeling melted into me. My pounding heart began to slow down. Amazingly, the boar stopped snorting, he just slowly turned and walked away into the blackness of the forest. He was gone, but my mind quickly imagined that there could be more. I now wanted to go home and kept thinking that I should have listened to my parents in the first place!

My eyes scanned the dark forest in all directions. I was lost and very frightened. As I looked for some escape, I began to see the most beautiful *gossamer, shimmering lights,* all around me. They were alive with sparkling rainbows of golden glow, feathered with soft pinks and greens. I had never seen such profound beauty in my life. Then, to my amazement, as I looked up to my right, I saw a tall, beautiful woman standing next to me. She was smiling sweetly, and I felt her love pouring into every part of my body, like warmed honey. I immediately knew it was a true Angel. Then, I felt a soft loving touch on my other shoulder and saw *ANOTHER* beautiful Angel standing on my left side.

"*I am lost!*" I said aloud. "We are with you, fear not my child. We will lead you out of the forest, you are safe now," they said with calm and reassuring voices. With the beautiful Angels at my sides, we walked slowly through the dark forest back to my home. I had never felt such love and safety at any time before in my life.

Daylight began to slowly appear as we walked hand-in-hand to the edge of the woods. I saw my backyard and noticed my mother's clothes still hung on the line. It was a relief, yet I did *not* want to go back! I wanted to *stay* with the Angels and *never* wanted them to leave my side! They both urged me to continue walking towards my home because my parents would be worried. Their final words were, "Someday, you will tell your story so others will be comforted in knowing *they are NEVER alone.*"

I thanked them for saving me and for all the Love I felt. I walked across the yard and up the apartment stairs, opened the door very quietly and tiptoed to my room. I never told anyone about this experience as I was too afraid that I would get into trouble. It was my secret. From that moment on, I knew that *I was never alone.*

HEARING AND SEEING FROM BEYOND

This was the art that hung over my bed as a child. I later had it reframed and hung it in son Kevin and Arie's room.

Bernhard Plockhorst (March 2, 1825–May 18, 1907) was a German painter and graphic artist. The Guardian Angel (1886) showing an angel and two little children close to the abyss, was reproduced as a color lithography in thousands of copies and greatly influenced the later pictures of guardian angels.

Chapter 2

Journey to the Dump Truck

"You can live your life angry, bitter, mad at somebody or even guilty, not letting go of your own mistakes, but you won't receive the good things God has in store."
—Joel Olsteen

I graduated from Ramona High School in Riverside, California and moved to Los Angeles when I turned 19. Having modeled for six years, I was now at the prime age to *make it* in the big world of fashion. New York was too far away, so off I drove to L.A. in my little white Valiant. Finding a small apartment with a fold down bed and a hot plate for cooking made me feel ready for success.

I was lucky enough to be hired as a staff model at I. Magnin, a high-end department store right across from Rodeo Drive. I was in the heart of it all. I worked with the top couture designers from around the world and wore clothes that had more zeros on their price tags than I had ever seen. It was a whole new world, and while I could write a book about it… I will just get to the most important points that led me on a more spiritual path.

I worked Monday thru Friday, from 8:00 a.m. to 4:00 p.m. and made a whopping $1.75 an hour. I was barely scraping by but knew that I was paying my dues and getting exposure for a career as a professional model. As a perk, I had the chance to wear clothes that cost thousands of dollars. I was learning more about modeling in the high-fashion world while, of course, dreaming of being discovered.

On my second week at the store, I was walking to the parking lot after work when a flashy bright yellow Ferrari pulled up in front of me. The fellow inside said he knew who I was because he knew my boss. He wanted to take me to dinner sometime. I quickly declined and said thank you. Then the bouquets of roses started showing up at my work with short, intriguing messages to entice me into going out with him. Finally, because of my innocence, I gave in to his male pressure.

While dating Mr. Yellow Ferrari, I lived in the fast lane, flying to Vegas after work and going to big parties with the jet setters. I ended up living with him and quickly lost my virginity. One day, *he* decided that I was going to marry him. I wasn't ready for marriage and tried to explain that I didn't yet understand what love was. To my shock, he told me that if I didn't marry him, he would have me so messed up that nobody would even want to look at me again. He clearly said that he was in the Syndicate (also known as the Mafia) with hit men who could do the job on me. I believed him as I actually met a hit man at one of our parties. To say the least, that both scared and woke me up, so I made my escape back to my mother's house in Riverside. I left him a note saying, *"This is your world and not mine. I wish you only the best."*

Thank God, after a year, he finally stopped harassing me and gave up his pursuit. I was an emotional mess, going from 127 pounds to 190 in about nine months. Smoking three packs of cigarettes a day and eating everything in sight, I used anything to push the fear and confusion down. I had no idea of who I was now that my dream career had crashed and burned. Later in life, I was grateful for the experience for it led me to search deeper into myself and ask, *"what is the meaning of my life?"*

I married Chuck few years later who became father to my first son, Chad. He was a kind and gentle man, but we both were too young to know what love really was, so we divorced after seven years together. We all mature in our own way, but my growth process always seemed to involve a man. I married from what I thought was love and gave it my best until I could give no more. I would then have to leave because growing together seemed impossible and my unhappiness became too great. Of course, it was *me* who needed to learn to love myself first. The journey to finding myself wasn't an easy path.

My second marriage was to a man named Jim. I remember thinking that we would evolve together, but I woke up one day realizing that we each move at our own pace. We mutually ended our relationship after three years. I still had not gotten the lesson about learning to love and accept myself fully.

I was later in my third and hopefully last marriage. My husband John and I had three homes, and I chose to live in the one in Idyllwild, California. I knew it was where I needed to be for my spiritual growth. As I turned 40, I had my sweet little two-year-old son Arie and I was pregnant with my third son, Kevin. Their father was an up-and-coming children's author, with engagements as a keynote speaker all over the country. He was in great demand and spent a lot of time away from home. For many reasons the distance between us became too much and we divorced when our boys were eight and eleven.

I believed in the fairytale idea of falling in love and living happily ever after and never gave up on the dream. I kept asking myself, *"Do I still believe in love?"* I truly did, but always fell into a role as a "giver," never knowing how to claim my own needs. This kept me stuck into a victim-tyrant consciousness dynamic. I would give everything for my husband's wants and desires until I realized that I was feeling lost and confused. After seeing two counselors for myself, I wanted him to join, but he was not open to the idea at that time.

John and I had been married for nine years when I reached my breaking point and left. The last words I heard from him were, "You are the only one with a problem in this relationship!" Something in me snapped. I loved who he was to the external world, but not who he was with me.

I moved half of the household belongings to our vacation cabin and left with the boys. Even though John refused my requests to do counseling, I left a note asking him to reconsider couples counseling. I had arranged a session with a neutral counselor and wrote down the time and date stating that this was the only way I would continue with him. The counseling was good for negotiating our separation needs, but emotionally, I was at the end.

About six months after our divorce, I had legal custody of the boys with a 50/50 living arrangement. The boys would spend one week with me and the following one with their father. Adjusting to a broken home and finding consistency with some semblance of order was a challenge for everyone. I was so sad and worried about how this was going to affect the boys.

ANGELS IN THE DUMP TRUCK

My boys were living with me in Idyllwild, California, and alternated house with their father's every other week. I was expecting them back from their week away, and it was getting past time for them to be home. Becoming concerned, I dialed their father's number, only to discover that it had been disconnected. When I called again, a sinking feeling filled my gut. The line was not in service and there was no new phone number provided. Something was very wrong. I drove directly over to the new home where their father lived with his new wife and walked onto the porch. I could see clearly into the front windows and only a few boxes were standing in the empty house. I was shocked! How could he just take the boys without discussing it with me first? I felt as if the air got knocked out of me. I couldn't believe my eyes! Where were they?

How could he disregard me so blatantly, I thought? My mind was racing as I drove back home. I yelled out loud, "Angels, show me where they are *now*! Do you hear me?" Then, to my amazement, I heard my angels say, "*San Juan Capistrano*." I ran upstairs, picked up the phone and dialed 411 for a new listing in that area. Sure enough, I was given his new number. I felt like I was watching an unbelievable movie. I dialed the number and *he* answered.

"What are you doing? How could you just move the boys without discussing it with me?" He started with a shocked voice, "Well, we decided it would be good for the boys to live at the beach." "*We?*" I answered, "*We* never included *me*! Even our divorce decree stated we had to give a 60-day notice to each other before moving off the mountain. I could call the Sheriff on you right now, but I do not want to upset the boys tonight. You must promise to bring them back up the hill tomorrow morning." He agreed.

When the boys arrived the next day, they told me how excited they were to have this new life. It looked like Disneyland to them, being close to the beach and next door to a park. They were concerned about me and how I would do without them.

Their father had already enrolled them in their new school. All this was done behind my back. My head was spinning. I didn't know if I should dig my heels in and fight or let them go. *How could he*? I was so confused and in shock. I did not know what to do. How could I just let them go? I finally told the boys I was going upstairs to meditate and ask God and the Angels for guidance.

I closed the door, lit a candle, and opened my meditation notebook. I prayed for all the Love of God, Christ, and my Angels to help me. I began to breathe through the aches in my body. I felt tied up in knots, especially in my heart. As I allowed myself to let go and become quiet, I began to feel more peaceful. The words I heard were "It is OK to let your boys go at this time. There will be things you cannot teach them that they will get by living with their father," the voice said. The tears were coming so fast I could hardly see and write in my book what I was being told. I was verbally reassured that my sons' love for me would only grow stronger because of my courage to let them go without fighting with their father.

"Who is speaking?" I asked. I understood it was Archangel Michael, although it was a bit hard to believe. I kept sitting in stillness for a long time. I became more peaceful about my dilemma as time passed. I stepped back, while still in meditation, and started to look at this situation from another perspective. I remembered how happy the boys were when John would return home from his many travels. They had this lovely bond, and he was a good father. I felt into this more deeply, knowing that I didn't want my sons to be in the middle of a custody fight. I wanted a good life for them, and I knew they could come back and live with me at any time if they desired. The boys really wanted to be with their dad, and I was getting clear guidance from my Angels to let this happen. When I was ready, I returned downstairs.

The boys turned off the TV and I shared with them that the Angels said it would be OK to let them go at this time. I reassured them that if, for any reason, they were unhappy and wanted to come back home, I would *always* be here for them. We all hugged and cried together. We were all reassured and shared how much we loved each other. I told them, *"I love you as big as the expanding universe."* They were relieved to know they could live with their father, but they could feel my pain as well. No one was completely happy about any of this.

Three difficult days had passed, and Kevin wanted to go to a thrift store called The Help Center. Why did he want to go there, I wondered? "Why not?" I said, "Sure, let's go, I have never been there. Who knows, we might find some treasures." As soon as we walked in, we heard employees complaining. "It's a shame...all that stuff going to the dump," one woman said. "I think it's a sin," another one replied. "That truck is just full of things we don't have time to go through or space to store." Kevin looked up at me and asked if they could go outside to see the truck. I thought the request was curious but said, "Yes," and off they went. A few minutes passed before Kevin came back in, took me by the hand and said, *"You are supposed to come out and see what's on the truck."*

He led me to the open bed pickup truck, piled high with clothes. Immediately I spotted a beautiful new pair of shoes, size nine and a half, and a perfect fit. My eyes also spotted a gorgeous jacket, my size, of course; one you would pay hundreds of dollars for at Nordstrom's.

The two workers were throwing more things on the truck. One looked towards us and said, "Take whatever you want lady, this is all going to the dump." My pile on the ground kept growing with so many treasures. I felt quite uncomfortable finding so much stuff.

I was leaning over to gather up my treasures when I heard a voice in my right ear say, *"Reach in and get the bag."* My next thought was, *"I am not reaching in for a dumb bag!"* The voice came in much louder this time, *"REACH IN AND GET THE BAG!"* All right, already, I thought! I climbed on the side of the truck, reached in and grabbed a grocery-sized bag from the mound of discards.

Arie and Kevin stood next to me as I reached into the bag. I pulled out an 8x10 picture frame. It was the classic image of an Angel watching over two children crossing the rickety bridge. This was the exact same picture that was beside my bed as a child, and which was now reframed and hanging in the boys' room. The second I touched the picture, I heard an immediate message, "The Angels are with you and your children. Fear not. You are not alone. Everything will be fine. Write your book about being lost in the Black Forest." Kevin immediately said, "See Mommy, our Angels are with us again!" My tears flowed with gratitude and amazement.

Arie took the picture as I reached into the bag again. This time I pulled out a beautiful silver crucifix of Christ on the cross. Again, there was an immediate message, "It is the time of rebirth, Janice. Just trust." I was amazed! I handed it to Kevin as I reached in a third time to find two greeting cards. The first one was from a Catholic Monastery. On the outside it said, in bold gold letters, "Passionate Spiritual Gift." When I opened it, we saw a beautiful colored picture of Jesus pointing to his heart with golden beams shining out. The second one was an Easter greeting card with the heading, *"Christ is Risen."* The inside blessing read, *"May the Risen Christ Fill your Heart with Joy,"* next to an image of Christ looking up with his hands held out. The time of rebirth was certainly clear.

Reaching in the bag again, I pulled out two little pouches with well-worn rosaries. One was glass beaded and the other was made from wooden beads. The message I heard was, "Just keep praying Janice. Your prayers will be answered." Kevin quickly said, "There's still something in the bag mommy." It looked empty, but I felt a strange little object. Sure enough, it was a small statue of Archangel Michael standing on the fallen Angel, the Devil, holding a long spear pointed at his head. Oh my God, Archangel Michael, who came to me a few days earlier to reassure me about the boys. I was strangely relieved by this confirmation. I was asking and praying for a sign that I was in the right direction. I had just received more than I ever could have imagined!

These were the treasured items I found on the dump truck:

FEELING ALONE IN AN EMPTY NEST

It was exceedingly difficult to adjust to an empty nest. I missed my boys terribly. I felt lost, alone, and deeply betrayed by their father. My life was turned upside down. I was looking forward to spending quality time with my boys every other weekend and on extended visits during school vacations.

Another part of my healing was done through transformational breath work using the Clarity Breathwork modality. By diving deeply in the process, I was able to peel many layers of pain and limited beliefs. That level of healing and insight was so powerful that it inspired me to become a certified practitioner. As I became more at ease, I learned to trust myself and my connection to Spirit more deeply. It led me to a journey through various forms of personal counseling and Spiritual Studies with Dr. Reverend Betty Jandal, the minister at the Center for Spiritual Living in Idyllwild, California. I became focused on my work as a Healing Facilitator and on finding new ways to balance my upturned life. Over time, I learned to trust life even more deeply.

Four years passed until I met Mitchell, a man who reminded me much of my first husband, kind and gentle. Yet, two years into our new marriage, we realized that we were both on different paths. He wanted to retire as a retail manager and live in northern California where his daughters lived, and play a lot of golf, which was his passion. I wanted to stay in my spiritual community and continue my healing practice in Idyllwild, two hours away from my sons. My heart was broken, and I thought I would never heal. I cried like never before and could barely stop because I truly believed that I could make this relationship work. I thought this was my last chance at *love*. Why we never had this lifestyle conversation before we got married still puzzles me. I guess I was *still learning!*

I went deeper into learning to love, trust, and forgive myself, again, for my bumpy journey. I continued to live on the beautiful mountain top of Idyllwild for a total of 25 years. I was blessed to be there, and I knew it.

As years passed, I had to ask myself if I really did believe in love. After all the heartache I had been through, it was a very valid question. A dear friend of mine, Uki MacIsaac, had come to stay with me following an Angel workshop. I wanted us to tune in together and ask the Angels the following question, "Should I stay open to meeting my true love or just shut the door and just get on with my life as a Healing Facilitator?" I will never forget what happened after we both became still and went within. The question was asked powerfully, out loud, and Uki quickly said, "They say he's just around the corner." "What corner?" I asked. We waited and listened…then I added, "Should I stay open to the option of meeting him online?" We both felt a big possibility did exist, so I chose to stay open and believe in love!

The next day I went to a dating site I had been using. While I had met interesting men, I felt they were not a fit, so I now knew myself enough to hit the delete button and move on. I had paid the service for three months, hoping to find my dream man, and my time was up in a couple of days. It was now or never! I sat comfortably, looking out at the expansive view from my desk, lit a candle, and then I loudly blurted out, "OK Angels. If I am supposed to meet the man I am looking for, then BRING HIM TO ME NOW! I HAVE HAD ENOUGH!" And I meant it with all my whole being. My declaration even shocked me. To my amazement, I was on the phone "with him" fifteen minutes later! (Yes, that deserves another exclamation mark!) Interestingly enough, he had been on the same dating site for only a week, and I was his first and last date.

Many years have passed, and I am now happily married to my "online husband," Bryan Bagley. We love adventures, and decided to go camping in Conception Bay, 650 miles south of the U.S. border in Baja California Sur.

I needed to get away to write and I knew this place was going to be the perfect location to start this book. It required a willingness to go deep into my emotions, to be vulnerable and to meditate with an openness to listen. The writing journey began while huddled up on the edge of the beach, braving a cool windy day, under a palm frond palapa. Covered with jackets, blankets and my dog's bed over my feet trying to stay warm, I am now ready to share my story. As Bryan brings me a cup of hot tea, I will now continue…

Chapter 3

Kevin's Passing

"When a child dies, you bury the child in your heart."
—Korean Proverb

Kevin was the youngest of my three sons. He was a loving young man who was well liked by his friends and teammates. He played soccer while growing up and water polo in his Junior and Senior years of High School. He was almost 25 years old when he took his life. This is my journey through the events that followed.

Three days had passed since Kevin's shocking and agonizing death, and my suffering became intolerable. I do not know how to describe the shock, but it is something we can all relate with in some way. I could not believe that my baby was suddenly gone. Part of the deep agony I was experiencing was mostly the shock that it was HIS own choice. I just could not wrap my mind and heart around that thought.

I finally decided to follow Bryan's suggestion and tried to settle down and meditate. In the turmoil, I needed to center myself and *allow the Love in*. My Angels had guided me to use breath work in a process I called *The Infinity Love Process*. It has been a big part of my personal practice for many years. This is an eight-minute method of grounding and opening into a place of receptivity using breath. As a teacher, I guided many others through this meditation. Now, amid all this shocking pain, breath would help me once again find some *centering* and *peace*.

As my mind and heart raced, I finally slowed myself down and proceeded to write my opening prayer at the top of a page in my meditation notebook. Surrounding myself in Golden Beams of Light, I called in God, Christ, My Angels, and Guides. I then found myself writing, *"And my Kevin in Heaven."* I then remembered a simple little song I would sing to him… "Kevin, Kevin you're from heaven." My tears now flowing, it was time to breathe and continue letting go.

Immediately after breathing and moving into stillness, I felt Love. "I Love you Kevin," I said out loud and with amazement, I thought I heard his voice reply, "I Love you too Mamma." My two other sons have never called me mamma quite the same way as Kevin did. He had a fast pace with a certain intonation. "Was it really him?" I wondered. Then I heard him again, "Yes Mamma, it's me, and I am so sorry!"

I was feeling Kevin standing in front of me, holding both of my arms with a very firm grip. Kevin's presence was strong, loud, and clear and so was mine! It was really amazing to later notice black and blue imprints where his thumbs were holding my arms. Those remained visible for almost two weeks!

That first connection between us was tearful and deep. It is the only communication that I choose ***not*** to share openly.

Once I accepted the reality of my son Kevin's death, I knew that the best place to have his memorial was in Idyllwild, where he spent his early childhood. This is a small community of great people with caring hearts. So many people came to help, including former teachers, school friends and the boys Kev had grown up with. In meditation, I heard, "prepare for 300." I had now learned to listen and follow my guidance. The immediate challenge was finding where to hold the service for such a large group. This was not an easy task in such a small town. After a couple of days, my dear friend Phyllis had found a church retreat facility. There was enough indoor seating and media equipment which could facilitate an event this size. Because of all the love and support around me, I knew it was way more than me working to bring this together. When looking back at these days, I am amazed at how much focus I had to coordinate everything I needed to do. It was all about honoring Kevin and I had to keep it together. I kept reminding myself that I could fall apart later.

Over the following days, I became caught up in all the *'doingness.'* (This word is not in the dictionary, but I will use it anyway. My boys always said that I should create an "according to mom" dictionary, as I was always making up such words.) What I mean is, I had been so busy doing phone calls, emails, notices in the Idyllwild Town Crier newspaper, and with so many details to bring Kevin's memorial together. I now needed to center myself again, so I closed the door, turned off the phone and opened up to any support that wished to come through from the other side. I was a bit anxious, wondering if I could possibly connect with Kevin again. Maybe he had moved on or was busy somewhere else. Perhaps he was dealing with his own journey on the other side. I just didn't know, so I had to trust and let go, yet I still wanted to try. I finally began breathing, dropped into the quiet and then, to my amazement, there he was again! Thank God I had learned to silence my mind and listen.

Our dialogue continued and I started writing our discussions using **K–** for Kevin's voice and **M–** for me (Mom). I knew that three days later I would be sharing this conversation at his memorial. I wanted it to be *real* and didn't want to sugar coat anything. Kevin also wanted this.

October 1, 2015

OH MY GOD!

M–"God Day, yes, even on this day. Oh my God, Kevin shot himself in the head and is brain-dead! I ask God, Christ and all our Angels of Love to be with us now!"

"I want to hear you, Kevin! I can listen! Let me breathe first then please talk to me if you can. I Love You. Please Forgive Me. Thank You. After following my Infinity Breath process for eight minutes and dropping into *stillness*, I heard his voice…"

K–"I love you Mommy! I am so sorry. Please forgive me."

M–"Let's rest together… You are now with the Angels. You are not alone, and I know you are feeling my love. I love you, Kevin. I am so sorry. Please forgive me for any part I played in your sadness. Feel my Love. I am still working on forgiving you for doing this to yourself. *I will get there* because I know forgiveness heals… Let us rest together. Be at peace my Kevo. You will always be my sweet baby and I will always hold you in my heart, even though I can't physically hold you anymore."

I spoke out loud and prayed, "Dear God, take my son's pain away. Help him to heal his spirit; help him to grow, learn the lessons he now needs to learn and help him to smile again. Help my heart to heal and find my voice of love. Take this pain away… I give it all to you Dear God. I put him in your hands. Surround me in your Grace. Help me to know I am not alone, thank you God."

I clearly heard Kevin's voice. We had connected and then I slipped into a deep sleep.

October 4, 2015

I JUST WANTED PEACE!

M–"God Day! I ask for the Golden Light of Christ Energy to surround me and my three sons Chad, Arie and Kevin. I ask you, Kevin, to be with me now. I will stop all the calls and the drama to *breathe*. Let us just feel love and peace together, and then, if you want to share anything with me, I will listen. Thank You."

"Is that you holding my right arm? I can feel you, but I can't hear you… Speak up."

K–"It's OK, Mom. It's OK. I want you to find peace. I want you to know how much I love you."

M–"I do."

K–"I love you Mommy. I just wanted peace. I am so sorry."

M–"Yes, Kevin I know you do. I tried so hard to reach out by sending you phone messages, texts, and pictures. I wanted you to connect and let you know that I was thinking of you and share how concerned I was for your happiness. That's all, I just wanted to love you and you shut me out!"

K–"I know, Mom. I was just trying to work out my life and wanted you to be proud of me."

M–"I was always, always proud of you, Kevin. Who you *were and are now* forever more is Love. Your soul came in with Love. Everyone could feel and see it. All your friends, and especially Arie, saw that you were the life of the party, the one that made everyone laugh."

"The love that you *are* lives deeply in the hearts of those you have touched. I knew you wanted to be here. I just didn't know it would be for such a short time."

"You are a special soul who flew in on a star. Maybe I never told you this little story... The night you were conceived, your father asked me if *we were safe*. We were using the rhythm method of keeping track of my cycle for birth control. I calculated my dates, and I believed that yes, we were safe. After we made love, your dad was looking out the window and said with amazement, "Oh my God, that was the *largest shooting star I have ever seen!*" I immediately wondered if I had the dates right. I *knew* you wanted to be here, and you were making your entrance known. The following morning was Super Bowl Sunday, and I remember how the thought of drinking any alcohol triggered a nauseating feeling. I checked the calendar again, and my recollection of the dates was off. I imagined that you came in and erased my memory banks so you could have your grand moment of arrival on a shooting star!"

"I am deeply sorry that you were feeling so much pain and pressure in life, and that you saw no other way through them. I only hope that I can become stronger from this and reach out beyond my pain of such a great loss, which is beyond what words can express. I hope to remind others that we are not alone. There is so much help available. We have all been given free will here on this earth plane to reach out from our aloneness, pain and loss and accept help."

"My mind runs to '*if only...*' *If only* you had reached out! You could have called a suicide hotline. They might have been able to help. *If only* you had reached out to a friend, to your girlfriend, to your brother Arie or to your oldest brother Chad... You would have felt all the love they have for you. *If only* you had reached out to me, I would have encouraged you and let you know that the problems you were feeling were only temporary! *If only* you had reached out for professional help... You would have realized that your feelings of failure and overwhelm about quitting your job and having no direction, or for experiencing situations you could not handle, were *never permanent*."

"Kevin, I will never totally understand. I just want you to be at peace. I want all of us to be at peace. I know, with your strong and beautiful heart, you want that too. I pray you find peace that surpasses all human understanding. I pray that you feel all our love, and that you *Rest in Peace, my Dear Son. Rest in Peace.*"

The following days I centered myself and created his Memorial. I don't know how anyone can think clearly when putting a funeral together, especially when feeling the confusing shock of such a tragic death. The image of his bandaged head, as he lay comatose in the hospital with brown paper bags taped to his hands, will be a horrid memory that will always be with me.

October 10, 2015

NO HOPE!

M–"OK Kevin, God, the Angels… Christ is with us now. Is there something you want to say? Speak up! I am listening." (I was mad!)

K–"I love you, Mommy."

M–"I know, I love you too. How are you doing?"

K–"Better than you, right now."

M–"I know, this is so hard. I miss you so very much."

K–"I am right here."

M–"But I can't ever hold you…yet I feel you hugging me. Your loving and strong presence is felt."

LOVE NEVER DIES

K–*"Keep breathing, Mom!"*

M–"Yes. Is it OK to share parts of our conversation with others?"

K–"Yes."

M–"What do you want everyone to know?"

K–"That I love them and I am so sorry for the way I shot myself in the head!" "I am sorry you and so many have *that* as a final picture of me."

M–"Yes, it sucks."

K–"I see that. It's awful Mom, and I am so sorry."

M–"I hear you, Kevin. I have gone through hundreds and hundreds of pictures because Chad is creating a video presentation of your life. I saw clearly who you were, the sweet joyful loving person that everyone loved. I know who you are."

October 11, 2015

KEVIN'S MEMORIAL

The day of the memorial had finally come. Bryan helped me up to the stage, as I prayed for strength to be able to speak. I took a deep breath and slowly looked out at the many sad and loving faces. There were almost 300 people, family, and friends, who came to honor Kevin on this day. I seemed to gain strength from all their love and knew Kevin was right by my side. I took a deep breath and began…

I thanked Local Color (a women's acapella singing group I used to sing with) and everyone for coming to honor Kevin and our family.

"Just two weeks ago, on September 24, I was watching a movie at home with my husband Bryan when the phone rang. It was Arie, Kevin's brother, telling me he was on the way to Kevin's house where he lived with his girlfriend. His Dad, John, had received a text message from Kevin and was now afraid Kevin might have shot himself!"

"I screamed, *'Oh my God*, how far away are you, Arie?' 'Fifteen minutes away,' I think he said, with a very shaky voice. I love you Arie, drive safely. Call me as soon as you get there. I hung up and shouted out loud, *'Oh My God Kevin No! NO! Please Hang On! We All Love You! Just Hang in There! I Love You So Much, Kevin! Oh, Dear God, Help Him! Angels Gather Around Him!'"*

Looking up from my notes, I scanned the room, took a deep breath, and continued. "The next thing I did was call a Practitioner from Seaside Center for Spiritual Living, our church in Encinitas. She immediately started praying and notified everyone in the congregation to pray."

"It was a torturous 15 minutes. I would have to wait for Arie to arrive at Kevin's, so I quickly called John. He had received a text message from Kevin saying he loved us both and more... He just wanted peace and to call 911 so his girlfriend did not find him first. I can't even imagine the terror that must have ripped through John, now frantically driving back from Los Angeles towards Costa Mesa where Kevin lived. I am sure John will tell you in his own words..."

Feeling comforted by everyone listening, I continued... "When Kevin was found, he had shot himself in the head. We later found out he had packed up all his belongings, cleaned the house and more, trying to minimize the pain he knew he would be causing. He had placed a note on the door saying, **'DO NOT ENTER BEFORE CALLING THE POLICE!'** Sadly, his girlfriend did find him first. He was rushed to University California Irvine (UCI), where we all converged in hugs and tears, just hoping and praying that somehow, he would be OK."

"I waited a very long hour and a half to finally see Kevin. His head was bandaged and bloody. He was hooked up to all sorts of machines and tubes running in and out of him. I couldn't even hold his hands as they had brown paper bags taped around them. It had something to do with the police investigation. I could *not* believe what I was seeing…my sweet boy! What have you done? *Why? Why? Why?* 'This is so terrible what you did to yourself,' I thought. I leaned over and kissed his forehead telling him how much I loved him. I could *NOT* believe my eyes."

"The Doctor took us to the side and showed us the X-rays of Kevin's brain where the bullet had entered and exited. Then he said, 'I am afraid this is terminal. There is *no hope*, he is completely brain-dead. I am so sorry.'"

I needed a moment of silence before I continued. Speaking about this traumatic experience brought another level of pain but I knew it to be necessary, so I could *keep it real*. I took another deep breath as I pushed on…

"Our family gathered in the waiting room and decided to donate all his organs, knowing it would help other families. We found out later that he was one of the best donors they had as he was young, healthy, and had a strong body. Ironically, he saved many other lives."

"I am shocked beyond belief…if I did not know that we are souls evolving and learning how to be in a physical body and that there is only a thin veil between us and spirit, I could not even imagine how I would be dealing with this tragedy. From my first meeting with Angels in the Black Forest of Germany, I knew that I was never alone. My Angels told me that one day I would share that wisdom with others. I lived my whole life with Angels and that led me to learn how to still my mind and listen to the loving guidance which is always just waiting to bless me."

"I have heard Kevin's voice and he has shown me in countless ways that he is with me. The only thing that has helped me get through this was to breathe, listen and know he is with the Angels, and God loves him unconditionally."

"Kevin is right here with us today. His presence with us today is loud, clear, and strong. Who knew I would now be able to communicate with my own son?"

Tears filled my eyes, and I took a big gulp of air. I continued… "I never know when it might stop. I never know when he might be on to more important things on the other side, and I certainly don't want to hold or slow him down in any way. I am not sure what happens on the other side, so each time he comes through it is a gift, an amazing gift."

"I will share some of the conversations Kevin and I had these last few days. I will point to my heart when it is me talking, and I will point upwards for Kevin's voice."

Hand on my heart, I began…

M–"There are lessons for us all to learn, Kevin. I want you to be at *peace*! I want all of us to return to love and forgive each other for any issues, which are real or imagined."

I pointed upwards.

K–"I love you Mommy. I just wanted Peace! I am so sorry."

M–"I am just sorry that you were feeling so much pain and pressures in life, that you saw no other way, and did not reach out to *anyone* to help you."

K–"I see that. It's awful, Mom, I am so sorry."

M–"I hear you, Kevin. These past few days, I have gone through hundreds and hundreds of pictures, so Chad could do a media presentation of your life… You truly are the sweet joyful loving soul that everyone loved! I know who you are."

K–"I just couldn't find the *peace,* Mom. Everything felt too much. I wasn't making myself happy by my choices. My mortgage job was so much harder than I thought. Working with people in really desperate situations in their life, trying to refinance their house to get the money they needed was too hard. I wanted to help so much, but I felt like I was failing them. It was overwhelming for me. I even tried hard to support the other guys at work so they could keep going when they struggled."

M–"Kevin, you tried hard to pass your mortgage test. You tried so hard to make cold calls to people and got rejected. You tried hard to make the loans happen. You tried hard to love your girlfriend and be there for her family, taking care of things when her dad recently passed away. You *never failed.* You were just overwhelmed and *could not feel any hope.*"

K–"I just didn't feel like I was good for anyone. I was letting everyone down, my girlfriend, my boss, my co-workers, my dad, and you. I just wanted you *all* to be proud of me."

M–"I hear you and I feel you. I was always proud of you. All of us wanted you to be happy, to find a way, a job that you felt good about and where you were making a difference. The money was just the reward, so to speak, for bringing your goodness to the world. So, what if it wasn't that job? Many doors open and close in work and in relationships. Sometimes we must close them and trust there will be new ones that will appear. We have to muster the courage and faith in ourselves, and in God working through us, in us, and around us, when we cannot see that goodness is waiting for us. We all get down and think it's the end at times, but all I know for sure Kevin, is that you are loved unconditionally by me and by God. I gave you birth, but God makes it happen! You were a miracle of love and always will be. Do you hear me?"

K–"Yes, I get it now. The Angels are helping me integrate and navigate here on the other side. I am so glad you can hear me, Mom. I wish everybody could."

M–"I will remind them to breathe and let go…becoming still and *practicing the presence of love* just waiting for them, and maybe they too can begin hearing you."

K–"Yes, that's it, Mom, that's it! *Peace to all.*"

M–"Yes Kevin, and from all of us, *peace to you.*"

K–"Thank you, and thank everyone, and tell them I love them. Peace to all…"

"Breathe." I wrote this on the page so I would remember to breathe. When I came to this word, I forgot it was for me and said it out loud. I quickly looked up and everyone took a very deep and much needed breath as well. I could see the relief on their faces as their shoulders dropped with their exhale! It was such a powerful experience to witness 300 people with their hearts wide open. I will never forget it.

"This has been the most painful experience I could ever imagine, not just for me, his mother, but for all of us. Our family and I are grateful for being blessed with so much love. Thank you all again for being here."

Tears rolled down my cheeks as my eyes fell upon the loving faces, with tears as well, in front of me. I was feeling raw and vulnerable because of my open honesty. This tragedy was the deepest wound I had ever had. I felt and sensed that I had just cracked open the minds and hearts of so many here today. Many knew him in their own special way, teachers, ministers, work pals, family, and friends. They all saw his light. Now, we had gathered to say goodbye to Kevin, from one of his favorite places, the beautiful mountain top of Idyllwild, California.

It was important to me that his memorial gathering be real. So many young men and women in their mid-twenties came up thanking me for *being real*. They all wanted to know what really happened and why. I could not really answer that question fully. I could only give them what Kevin gave me; the reasons were deeper than anyone could understand. How could it be, Kevin? He was the one who lit up a room when he entered. *NOT KEVIN*!

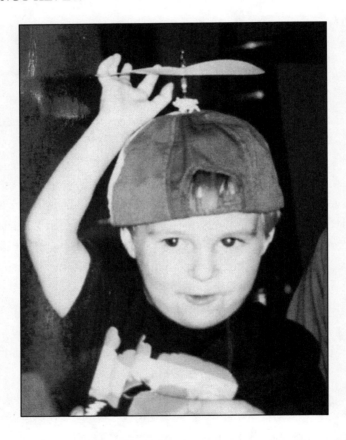

I was deeply moved by his playmates, now in their twenties. So many admitted that they also struggled to make sense of their life and felt they were missing a sense of direction. They had so much pressure to get it all together, I thought. I could feel these sweet young men were also struggling themselves under life's pressure. Something was awakened in them, and it shook them to their core. As they confided and thanked me, I reminded each one to reach out and to not hide. They should know how special they are and that there is *always help*! I believe this truth drove my desire to be real and to go beyond my deep grief and shock of losing my baby. I wanted Kevin's life to make a difference.

Ironically, this was the last gift I received from Kevin. It hangs in my office and makes me think of beautiful moments when he was acknowledging Angels as an important part of my life.

Chapter 4

Our Communication Continues

"The worst wounds, the deadliest of them, aren't the ones people see on the outside. They're the ones that make us bleed internally."
—Sherrilyn Kenyon

Following the memorial, I was still processing the mixed emotions from that day. I was thankful to have the support from my Angels and the wisdom and comfort they provided. As I asked for guidance, they confirmed that I should write this book which seemed important to Kevin. This encouraged me to continue documenting my discussions with him to share his message.

Oct. 14, 2015

M–"My dear Kevin, how are you doing up there?"

K–"Things are slowing down now. I guess you could call it resting. I'm feeling lots of love pouring into me."

M–"Do you still feel like you are in a body, in some way?"

K–"Yeah, but it's so much lighter. The *'doingness'* and the heavy feelings are gone."

M–"That's good."

K–"Lots of Angels and light surround me. There are souls who passed over before me here that I didn't know, like both my grandpas. So much love! It's hard to describe."

LOVE NEVER DIES

M–"Did the Memorial service help you?"

K–"Wow, Mom, it was awesome! So many people...all my friends. Idyllwild really came out to support you, Dad, Arie and Chad. Everyone was so awesome, and you rocked, Mom. I couldn't believe you did it so well. I was with you, right by your side, as you stood at that podium."

M–"Yes, I know, I couldn't have done it without you! Do you know how loved you are now?"

K–"Yes, Mom. I am just sorry it was so sad for you and everyone... I really am. That damn gun was too handy. It just made it too easy, but it was the hardest thing I ever did. I am so, so very sorry, Mom!"

M–"Yeah, me too. It is a pain I will always have to live with! I just wished you could have reached out and hung on. I am so sorry that you had such deep pain. Rest my dear, just rest."

"Tomorrow, while I'm under the anesthesia, maybe we can see each other? Who knows? Could you guide Dr. Westermeyer to do a good job on my left foot?"

K–"Sure, Mom, I will be there."

I was scheduled for surgery four days after the memorial. The timing wasn't ideal, but that date had been set months in advance. I had waited seven years to get my foot fixed, following a bad fall where I slipped down 15 icy stairs. I tried holding on to the railing, but my left ankle turned in and my right knee went out, as I bounced down, one stair after the next. While falling, all I could think about was *'don't hit your tailbone,'* as I had already broken it three times before. I had done more damage than I realized but gathered myself up and kept going.

My foot had no tendons and ligaments holding it except my Achilles tendon, which was always inflamed! My right knee was bone on bone.

OUR COMMUNICATION CONTINUES

Walking was difficult, to say the least. I put up with the pain until I couldn't stand it anymore, and finally had medical insurance. I knew I had to move forward and forget the pain for Kevin's Memorial, knowing that only four days later I would be facing this major surgery. It was comforting to know that Kevin was with me. He had shown a strong presence; it was now undeniable.

Oct. 16, 2015

ENCOURAGEMENT TO HEAL

K–"Hey Mom."

M–"Hey right back to you."

K–"Sorry you're going through this, Mom, but it will be so much better. You have a great doctor. I think he really did a great job."

M–"Were you watching?"

K–"Yeah, pretty cool, I was with you."

M–"I don't remember."

K–"That's OK, we're good."

M–"Yes, we are. You're out of the body form and I'm getting mine fixed. Kinda weird, right?"

K–"You have lots to do still, Mom. More talks you're going to do standing behind those podiums, up and down those stage stairs. Got to get in shape for all that. Yep! We're going to do it together. First, we must rest. Sleep with the Angels Mommy."

LOVE NEVER DIES

M–"You too, Kevo. I love you."

K–"Love you too."

Oct. 20, 2015

CLOSER NOW

M–"God Day, I now open and let go. I feel so strange being stuck in bed, on my back, and not able to walk. I want to open. I want to hear you. How are you, my Dear Kevin? OK? Speak up! I love you."

K–"Love you too, Mommy. Sorry you are hurting. I am right with you."

M–"I am so glad. You feel calmer. Is that right?"

K–"Lighter, I guess, is the best way to see that."

M–"Lighter is good."

K–"Yep! Wish I could help you."

M–"I feel that just your love and caring makes me feel more at peace. I'm learning to be patient and giving my body time to *heal the heel*. Glad we can still make each other smile, right?"

K–"Pretty cool."

M–"Yes, it is very cool. It's weird…now that you are in spirit, I feel closer to you than I did in the past year."

K–"Sorry Mom. I'm 'up' here now. I can help you from this side in the best way that I can, with bringing people together or the synchronicities

OUR COMMUNICATION CONTINUES

of life. I am really here to help, but *it's always up to you to ask first.* Remember that Earth is a freewill zone."

M–"Well, I am totally open for that, in every little or big ways. Seems like my friend Jill just arrived for a visit. Thank you, Kevin, it gives me great peace to know you are with me. I love you."

Oct. 21, 2015

THE GOD GLUE

M–"God day, Christ, my Angels, and my Kevin in Heaven. I will now breathe and open to your love and guidance. Thank You."

M–"I Love you Kevin."

K–"Hey Mom, Love you too."

M–"It really amazes me how we continue to hear each other. How do we do this anyway?"

K–"Well, it's the God Glue."

M–"The what?"

K–"The God Glue. It is because you forgive me."

M–"It took me a while to keep going deeper into the love I have for you. Going through the many feelings of shock, sadness, and anger that you have taken your own life and be willing to let it go. Kind of like peeling a strong onion that makes you cry, but you keep going and going until it all falls apart. Then I was freed up inside and all I had left was my deep love for you. Silly the onion part, but I guess you get it? I just kept staying with my feelings… I knew it was the only way through, so I would not be completely consumed by a darker place. I also asked your forgiveness for any part I played, consciously or unconsciously, that could have contributed to deepening your unhappiness."

K–"That's it, Mom. It is because we forgive each other and return to the Love where we are connected! That's the God Glue! It's the *Grace, the Magic of Love*."

M–"I love that and love how you see and phrase things. It is so you."

K–"Glad you get it, Mom."

M–"Yes, I do. I am so grateful we are both choosing to stay open with each other. I am learning a lot. Thank you and thanks for explaining the *God Glue*!"

K–"You got it, Mom. Love you."

M–"Love you too."

Oct. 22, 2015

THE GUN

M–"God day, Angels, Guides and Ascended Masters and my Kevin in Heaven. Help me to let go and find Peace and understanding on this day."

M–"I know you said it wasn't easy for you to end your life. I can't even imagine the thoughts and pain you must have had. Did having a gun around make it easier for you to not find other solutions?"

K–"Yes, Mom, you are right, nobody made me do it… *I did it*."

M–"*I know, honey, I know*. This is upsetting you. I feel it. I can't pretend it didn't happen and just forget it. There is no doubt this is painful for all of us left here and it sucks! I can't say what is right for you. You did it and now, there you are! NOT dead, just out of your body. Of course, I wanted you to stay and find happiness, but you felt trapped somehow. Now, you can still see and hear others and me from there. I am not sure how you find peace to go to the Light, but that is my wish and prayer for you. Let your Angels embrace you into Heaven, far from this earthly experience. I want you to be with me only if you can be fully embraced by God!"

K–"I am here. I'm so sorry that you're so sad."

M–"Stand firm in the Light, my love."

K–"I am, Mom. It's OK, really."

M–"I just want you to find happiness and peace. It's my job to do the best that I can here. I just want to make a positive difference."

K–"You are, Mom, and you will. I am on your team."

M–"Awesome!"

Nov. 1, 2015

TAKEN TO FLIGHT

M–"Are you there Kevin? Where are you on your Spiritual Journey? I love you."

K–"Love you too."

M–"You think you can help me to understand our journey of expansion? I would like to share our ability to communicate with others. Would that be a benefit to others and are you good with that?"

K–"Yes, Mom. I wish I could let everyone know how much we are all loved. You have good work to do down there, and I will help."

M–"OK, let's do this."

K–"You seem a bit tired, Mom? Healing that foot takes more energy than you think? How about you rest, and I will be with you in dream time?"

M–"Fine with me. I love you so much."

    As I drifted to sleep, I found myself being picked up by Kevin and held in his arms. My cheek turned to his chest, he kissed my forehead sweetly and told me to just let go. While I allowed this to happen, he asked me if I wanted to fly. "Yes," I said. And the next instant, we began to gently fly over a multitude of colored trees. They were more vivid than a stand of autumn trees in the countryside of Massachusetts. *Amazingly gorgeous and breathtaking.* Then we glided over a river that dropped off into a very steep canyon and we swooped down the waterfall to a beautiful rainbow below. I had no more conscious memory after that, just a wonderful sleep.
    I awoke remembering the incredible, sweet, and beautiful journey we had together. I never had such an experiential journey in dream time. Maybe it was real…and he took me to experience the beauty of Heaven? Is that possible, I wondered? Everything inside me seemed to be stretched so much further than I ever thought possible.

OUR COMMUNICATION CONTINUES

November 4, 2015

KEVIN, CAN YOU HELP?

M–"How are you doing, my dear? I love you, Kevin. It makes me so sad that you are not here. Can you cheer me up?"

K–"I know I'm not supposed to say I am sorry because we completely forgive each other, but I am so sorry Mom. I didn't know how much this was going to hurt you. I couldn't know. I see and feel you now, and I wish I could make it all better."

M–"I feel that, Kevin, I really do. I am listening. I felt you pick me up and fly over beautiful trees changing colors, waterfalls, and a gorgeous rainbow. It felt so healing. Can we do more of that? I am concerned about taking you away from more important things on the other side."

K–"It's OK. Remember, there is no time… It's hard to get that from there, right?"

M–"Right."

K–"So, no worries. Remember, I can be in many places at once. It's called being multidimensional. You are going to heal that foot and knee and I see you walking on the beach and playing Frisbee again. It's all going to be OK."

M–"Oh Kev, thank you for loving me so much. Nap time. See you there?"

K–"I'll be there. I love you Mamma."

M–"I love you too, big as the expanding Universe."

Chapter 5

The God Vibe

*"If you had any idea as to our true potential together
You would do most anything to acquire our conscious union.
We respond in full power to awakened Souls, and answer in
degrees to those beginning to awaken. We are completely
dedicated to you and can help you as you help yourselves."*
—Message from my Angels

As I struggled to navigate through the physical pain of surgery, I was also in the thick of the emotional pain of Kevin's passing. It was so shocking and heart wrenching, but fortunately, I was reminded by Kevin of the vast Love that was with me. His new perspective allowed him to start seeing how his ego had pushed away all the Love and any help and that was available to him.

November 5, 2015

REALIZING HE WAS NEVER ALONE

I opened, as usual, writing at the top of the page, "God Day, Christ, My Angels, my Guides, and my Kevin in Heaven." After breathing and meditation, I heard his voice…

K–"Hey Mom."

M–"Hey Kevin, what's up?"

K–"I am doing well. I want you to know you are loved by so much Love, I can't even describe it. But it's there right now with you, in you, and around you."

M–"I will slow down and let myself feel it deeply inside. Do you help direct it?"

K–"No, it just is. Now that I am on this side, I realize that's all that is. This Love, this *Light Energy* is endlessly creating more of itself, the God Vibe. It's so big, so beautiful, and so expansive."

M–"Sounds wonderful that you now know this. What can I do here to allow this God Vibe in?"

K–"You're doing it, Mom. Interestingly, you are in this healing phase and it's time to slow way down."

M–"Right."

K–"Write, Mom. Just keep on writing. It's all going to go out like a w*ave of Love,* and you are the channel for this Love. Write about the fact that we are not alone and loved unconditionally."

M–"I can feel you. I wish you knew this before…"

K–"You tried to tell me, Mom. You tried to show me. I remember when Arie and I saw the big light moving down the hall. I yelled, and you came running upstairs."

M–"Yes, at Verlaine's house in High Castle. It was the day we moved out of the house where we lived with Dad. I had moved some of our things to the Foster Lake House when he was away on a trip. I was so scared, sad and upset but it seemed the only way. I knew you and Arie were going through such a confusing time and were upset too. Mommy was leaving daddy; your world was turning upside down."

"I ran upstairs and held you both as you told me about a great big light moving down the hall. I knew it was an Angel that was trying to tell us that we were not alone. It was a wonderful sign. I reassured you both as I tucked you into bed, singing the *Bubble* and the *Angel* songs. I loved singing for you every night. You then both drifted off into a peaceful sleep."

K–"I remember, Mom. The Angels are here. They are with you right now, it's so cool."

M–"Yes, it is, honey… Beyond cool. Yet, it's hard to always remember that while we are here on earth."

K–"We are so much more than our physical and emotional pain, Mom.

If you're not doing something to slow down, you can get lost down that rabbit hole like I did. You need to breathe and open up to receive the Love, and messages of loving encouragements. I got lost in the struggles of life and I really didn't see any way through them. Now, I see that I gave up because I didn't use the tools to help myself. And when buried so deeply in perceived failures, the idea of asking for help never occurs to those suffering. It never crossed my mind that help was even available.

M–"Do you really see that you gave up too early and things might have gotten better?"

K–"*I do*…now, from where I was then, there was no way."

M–"I am so sorry, Kevin. I miss you so very much, but I am glad you can talk with me and hear me, and I can hear you. Like I've told many people, I never thought I would be able to hear you, *or that I would ever have to*. It's still shocking as heck, and I have to keep getting out of the way, yet bam; here we are."

K–"Just keep opening Mom. Just know I am right with you. Also, you are not stopping me from other important stuff. This is the important stuff, right now."

M–"How do you see yourself helping me give others hope and faith?"

K–"You're doing it right now, Mom, and we'll just do it together. Remind them they too are not alone and to hang in there… God will help them in so many ways. Stay open to love. Help is on the way. Healing is happening. There is always a way."

M–"OK my dear, I got it, let's do it. I am so proud of you. I am so much more at peace knowing *that you* know this. Thank you for choosing me to be your mother. I will always love you unconditionally. Peace."

K–"Love and peace to you, Mom."

November 17, 2015

JUST TRUST IN THE GOD VIBE

M–"I love you, Kevi. Can you help guide me to following my purpose in being here in this body?"

K–"Hi Mom."

M–"Hi Kev, how are you doing sweetheart? I miss you and I am still sad you are not here. It seems every time I open, you are there and each time I feel a bit better."

K–"I know, Mom. Me too. I care about you so much and I know you are tired of all the pain. It's hard to know you are in pain both physically and emotionally, but I know it's going to be better."

M–"What can you tell me about my direction, or about being in service to others? I know you said that you are helping, but it seems like people are suffering so much right now. What do you see from the other side that could help?"

K–"Mom, *it's all about trust and Love.*"

M–"Right, tell me more."

K–"Trust that your body is healing and all the love and support you need is, and will be, there as you need it. Lots of things are coming together on many levels, but that *is* what's happening right now. So, trust that you are saying yes to love at the deepest levels, in all ways. When you think you are just stuck in the pain, you are limiting energy flow and not allowing this good healing vibe in."

M–"I see and feel that. I love you referring to it as the God Vibe.*"

K–"Right! That's why, when you breathe or meditate, and intentionally open to it, you begin to feel better and better.

M–"I'm glad I have got so many tools to use. It's just moving our past-conditioned self out of the way and using breath, then bam! Here is the God Vibe, here is the Wisdom and here is the Love. I am so thankful and grateful."

K–"Me too, Mom, I love you so much. I want you to be happy, to share these messages and all that you know, and what you are willing to learn, with others. You know a lot, Mom. You have learned more than you realize. The more you are willing to write down, the more you will see."

M–"You sound quite confident, Kevin."

K–"I'm down with that, Mom. We all make a difference, even though I didn't think I was making a big enough difference, I was. Know that you are loved bigger than the expanding Universe, Mom. Not just by me, but by the Love that is so big and ever expanding. It's so incredible, so amazing, that words will always be too small to use as a description. Just trust!"

M–"Love you too."

MY PERSPECTIVE ON THE GOD VIBE

I would like to expand on what Kevin is referring to as the God Vibe. When you are in emotional pain, you feel blocked. The thoughts go round and round, with no relief. Instead of feeling better, you keep going down a rabbit hole, which is limited thinking. The mind makes up all sorts of stories to justify why you are miserable. That story seems to grow, and it settles inside you, making you feel heavier. There seems to be no way out and from this vantage point, there's not. Things only look and feel worse. A shift can only happen when you desire a change and are willing to go through to the other side of your pain. Accept where you are, and then ask for help. Next, trust that you will be helped. Stay away from making up any more stories and breathe. **The first key is to consciously want and choose to feel better.**

Because we are created from Love, we are surrounded by many forms of this Love. We have help coming to us as loving messengers from God, Christ, our Angels, Guides, or a wise friend at the perfect time. Endless possibilities are opened. We have loved ones from the other side, that wish to be of service, and help with our journey. When we allow ourselves to be open to receive, this can go much further than just guidance. When we trust and let go, an energetic shift happens. We are then able to feel a deeper sense of ease, or a melting of tensions that we have been holding in our body. The shoulders begin to relax and the chest area around the heart starts to expand. Opening to the vibration of pure love brings us into the wholeness of who we are. *Healing happens because we open to it.* We have aligned ourselves with the truth of revealing who we really are… Love. We are spiritual beings gifted with the experience of living in a body.

After the reconstructive surgery on my foot and ankle, I was in a lot of physical pain. Being cut open and fixed with wires and screws was very uncomfortable, but I knew this disruption in my body was only temporary. I was in a healing phase, not only physically but emotionally. I knew to not run away from physical pain or from the deeply felt sadness of losing Kevin from this world. I could have chosen spiritual bypass, pushing away the emotions and just trusting that everything would be OK, but I knew the importance of staying true with this deep loss. *I had to go through the feelings*, and acknowledge the pain, in order to experience deeper healing at all levels.

I was in the rawness of my intense agony; I took a deep breath to allow the God Vibe in. I let my awareness and attention from my pain move up through my heart and then higher to the top of my head. This breathing went up from my heart throughout my body and I released each breath upwards. As I kept doing this, I was opening and feeling ease with each breath. My awareness began to move up and the deepest feeling of peace and ease would move in. I was opening to a very deep Love. There was a profound release of emotional and physical pain. This energy, almost indescribable and difficult to put into words, is then brought down into the heart where it continues to radiate through the entire body. I guess that's why I like Kevin's terminology, referring to it as The God Vibe. It is simply put, yet it means so much. I can say for sure that Love is always waiting and forever here for us all. It is our choice to simply open to receive. You can do this in a moment by taking a deep breath and simply letting it in. Just try it!

November 19, 2015

LIFE REVIEW

M–"I love you, Kevin!"

K–"I love you too, Mommy."

M–"So, what's happening?"

K–"Reviewing."

M–"Your life?"

K–"Yes."

M–"What have you learned?"

K–"I was a good person."

M–"Yes, I know that. You always were such a joy."

K–"Yeah, there are things I need to forgive, but it's not done instantly. I have to really feel it to let it go."

M–"Well, we've already been through this, but I totally forgive you for not reaching out to me in the last year. I understand you were doing it your way. Even though it made me sad, and I missed you so much."

K–"Right."

M–"It's just weird because I always felt we had such a special bond."

K–"You are my Mom and I am so glad. I wouldn't want anyone else. I mean that Mom. You love me unconditionally and that's the best I can have. It really helps me so much to know you can hear me and feel my love."

M–"Ditto! It is a gift I am still letting in, a gift of your unconditional love to me. A gift God has given us, and it goes beyond words into the deepest feelings of Love and connection. This is so amazing and wonderful."

K–"I know you hear my thoughts, just like my voice, and sense my feelings. I also feel yours. It's the God Vibe between us."

M–"It's a beautiful thing. It's deep and light."

K–"Glad you are able to get up and around more but don't overdo it, Mom."

M–"OK, I'll be careful. Keep loving and learning, Kevin, and know I love you."

K–"As big as the expanding Universe?"

M–"Right."

November 28, 2015

ASKING FOR HELP

M–"My Kevin in Heaven, I love you, be with me now. Were you with us last night at the pizza gathering?"

K–"Yes, it was good to see you all together having fun with the new pizza oven Bryan built."

M–"I was talking with Arie and Chad about the day when they took your body for organ donation. They were both at the hospital, but I just *couldn't* go again. It was too much! I knew you weren't in your body anymore as you were with me. They then drove to our house in Encinitas where I was so comforted to see them. I asked both, "Why did you think that Kevin wouldn't reach out to me? Why is it so difficult to ask for help? We are not alone, there's always help." Arie replied, "We love you so much, Mom, and we don't want to share that we're not doing well. We just want to call when we have only good things to share. I guess it's a matter of pride and a guy thing. Pride Goeth Before the Fall."

K–"From my new perspective, I realize there's nothing wrong with asking for help. I don't know why it's so hard for people on the earth plane to ask for help when so much guidance, Love and support are just waiting to be offered. Maybe it's a God set up. Once help is asked for, and people have learned to wait and surrender, they will then feel the shift, the grace and the synchronicities which just weren't coming together before."

M–"I think that's right, Kevin. Why we push love away is most puzzling and painful. Maybe it's about learning how we are all connected?"

K–"Yeah, it's very cool, very amazing. I just wish I could have learned this before…"

M–"I know, my dear. Forgive yourself and love yourself. Allow all the Love and *Light of God's Power* to be with you now and forever more. You are loved so much by all of us.

M–"I just received the news that the donor recipients of all your organs are doing well. Did you know you were going to help others live? I feel like that gave you some strength, am I right?"

K–"Yes, Mom, and I have been with all the people who received my body parts. I'm helping them to heal and be at peace with accepting me in them. Sounds kinda weird, but I want them to live because they also want to live. It is wonderful to see the families happy, especially at Thanksgiving. I am grateful that I could make a difference. I really am."

M–"Yes, me too, my dear son. I love you bigger than the expanding Universe.

K–"I Love you too, Mommy. Rest now. Let's fly…"

December 3, 2015

THE GOLDEN CORD

M–"Love you Kevin, in Heaven. Can you see the sick and suffering, not just the people you love, but others on the planet? I feel you holding my left arm. Thank you for coming through so strong. How are you feeling dear?"

LOVE NEVER DIES

K–"I'm good. It's not boring here, that's for sure. I am still surrounded by my Angels, and I have traveled all over. It's like this... I can see it all, but my focus is more on my family and friends right now."

M–"Understand."

K–"Remember, Mom, death is an illusion. Spirit in each of us is eternal."

M–"Right, I got that. It is hard for me to see terrorists feeling such anger and then killing innocent people."

K–"They are set free by God's Grace. Even in the worst of times, God's Love is present to lift them to a new level of awareness."

M–"I hear that, and it's hard to remember when someone you love is just gone; when they're not here to love, hold and laugh with. It brings tears to my eyes and makes me cry just feeling how much I miss you, and yet, here I am having this interaction with you."

K–"I feel your sadness, Mom, I do. I can't take that away and I am sorry. *Love never dies*, though! Love is forever and always. It's like a Golden Cord that will forever hold us on Earth as it is in Heaven."

M–"I guess that is the beauty of love. As you shared that, my sadness and tears turned into gratitude that this *is* true. Love is who you are Kevin, and I am so glad that you are my Kevin in Heaven. Love you big as the expanding Universe."

K–"Love you too."

December 22, 2015

CHRISTMAS MESSAGE

M–"God Day, Christ, my Angels, my guides, and my Kevin in Heaven. It is a time of coming together in Love and being grateful for the birth of Jesus. I am concerned about Arie. I am missing Kevin. I will breathe; I will let go. I ask for all the Love to be with me now. Can you help, Kevin?"

K–"Hey Mom, Merry Christmas."

M–"Hey Kev, Merry Christmas to you. I was wondering if there are any celebrations in Heaven?"

K–"Some do if it makes them happy."

M–"Not everyone in Heaven celebrated Christmas here on earth."

K–"Right, but the choirs of Angels sing to the Light He brings to earth."

M–"Wonderful, I wish I could hear it. It makes me think of the song *Gloria in Excelsis Deo*. Oh, Kevin, I miss you so much. I am grateful for all the Christmases we had together. I loved that you would always help me with decorating the Christmas tree. It was great fun for me to have the presents wrapped and waiting under the tree. I loved the days of a white Christmas, sledding down the hill next to our house, and hear you screaming with joy when you would catch air flying so high. I'm very grateful for that time together."

K–"Me too Mom, I wish it would be that way every day. Nothing and no time can ever take that away. We will always have that."

M–"Wow! That is true, isn't it?"

K–"Yep, life had its good times and lots of them. Thank you, Mom, for always making it special for us…all the presents and a tree every year. I loved it. You were the one who always made it happen. It was you who brought it all together in every way. I love you for that, Mom. I am sorry that makes you cry. I know you miss me. I am with you."

M–"Yes, I feel you and know you care. I am grateful through the tears, I really am. Do you have any advice for me to help Arie?"

K–"Love him."

M–"I do, so much, but he seems to block me out and it feels like he's getting further away!"

K–"He has to do it for himself. Just don't be afraid of letting him know you are here for him. I heard you every time, Mom. With every text message and every voice message, I knew you loved me. I just wanted you to be proud of me when I wasn't feeling it for myself. I would run the other way, like running into my bedroom as a child when I was sad or mad, remember?"

M–"Running away is what you did as a boy, and you simply continued to do as a young man. I would always reassure you and let you know how much I loved you. You always seemed to get it and came back out with an open heart.

K–"Right."

M–"I'm just going to continue reaching out to Arie, love him unconditionally and trust that he's going through his own life process."

K–"Tell Arie this message from me, 'I love you Bro! You are the best brother I could have had! Now, let me help you be the best you can be. Let in the Love. I am so sorry you are sad and that I left you, but I am here for you. Our love will never end—never. Mom, Dad and Chad love you. *Let in the Love!* I wish you a Merry Christmas Bro.' And Merry Christmas Mom and Bryan. Tell him thanks for loving my mom and for taking good care of her. Be happy that you have three sons who love you. You're the best."

M–"Thank you Kev. Merry Christmas to you. Thank you for your Love. I promise to share this with Arie and Bryan."

K–"Thanks Mom. *I LOVE YOU ALL SO MUCH! BE HAPPY AND DON'T WORRY!*

January 3, 2016

FREEDOM OF CHOICES

M–"I Love you, Kevin. Are you with me?"

K–"Yeah Mom, I am here… I've been with you."

M–"I am not always quiet enough to listen. Sorry."

K–"No worries."

M–"What are you doing?"

K–"I am expanding my awareness and looking at how my life with each person affected them. Noticing the challenges they are facing…observing with love from this side. I am realizing and seeing all the Love around and with them. I'm wishing that they all knew this right now so they wouldn't limit themselves and would love their life. It's a great opportunity to have such freedom to make your own choices. I am just amazed how limited people think they are."

M–"I hear that. I guess it's always about choosing limitation or expansion with every thought, right?"

K–"Yep, and sometimes those thoughts that appear to run us feel more real than the more uplifting thoughts that free us. Crazy, right?"

M–"Right! It seems like the work here is all about our awareness."

K–"Glad you know that, Mom. I can see you are working on that with lots of things. You'll get through it."

M–"Thanks for your love and support. I'm going for a ride to Julian with Bryan, care to join us?"

K–"Good to get out. Love you, Mom."

March 21, 2016

GENIE IN A BOTTLE

M–"Kevin, Kevin, come in from Heaven…"

K–"Hi Mamma."

M–"Hello my dear, it's been a while. It has been hard to tune in while in pain with two fractured ribs and the shock of needing to have a second surgery for foot and ankle. I am always afraid that if I go too long between our sessions together, you might think I am not interested in listening or that you will have moved on."

K–"No, Mom, it's OK. I really am here. It's so cool that your garden is coming alive on this first day of spring. I love the roses!"

M–"So, what's going on for you?"

K–"I am going to a deeper place of reflection as I do expansion work. I see and understand more clearly the pressures I felt and my inability to deal with my frustrations. It's easier to see from here while looking back. I do miss you, Mom, but I am here for you and always will be. Just ask and I'll be like the *Genie in the Bottle,* coming out to grant your wish, if I can help in any way."

M–"That is wonderful Kevin. I am truly grateful that you love me so much. I so wish I could give you a big hug right now. So energetically, I will with all my heart. I love you, Kevin."

K–"I love you too Mommy."

Chapter 6

A Life Shortened

*"But there was no need to be ashamed of tears,
for tears bore witness that a man had the greatest
of courage, the courage to suffer."*
—Viktor E. Frankl, author of
Man's Search for Meaning

Death is part of the life cycle, and we usually don't have the conscious ability to choose when the departure out of our body will happen. Being asked to support a friend transition to the other side was a true honor and Kevin's presence was very clear.

April 4, 2016

HEALING HERE AND THERE

K–"Hey Momma."

M–"Hey Kevin, nice to hear and feel you. Thanks for the yellow roses. I am a bit confused whether I should stay here or go on a trip to Mexico with Bryan. I haven't been out on any adventures since all my surgeries began seven months ago. So much pain got me down a bit."

K–"I wanted you to feel the Love. I'm sorry you're having a hard time. It's my fault, I know it. I am sorry it hurts so much missing me. I really am. You are on the right path of feeling it by allowing all the feelings of sadness move through you. Don't be afraid to feel it fully, Mom. I was not willing to feel, and it sure didn't work for me to run away and stuff it. Don't hide from others either, like I did."

"I think you should go to Mexico. I am with you and you're not going without me. Feel the peace there, meditate and write. Just be with the stillness and the beauty all around. Your friend Sharon who wants you to go needs you there. You don't have to stay here in your bedroom to feel and hear me. It just doesn't work that way. I think you need to go. You will feel better, I promise."

April 6, 2016

LOVE YOUR LIFE TRUST

M–"God day Angels, Guides, and my Kevin in Heaven. We made it to San Felipe Mexico and are staying with friends. It was kind of hairy with the truck accelerator going dead on the highway while we were driving. I am sure you helped us by sending the best and most caring Spanish-speaking man who came to help us. Thank you for getting us here. I will now breathe and let go… Any guidance?"

K–"Glad you made it, Mom."

M–"Me too! Thanks for all your guidance and support."

K–"You got it Mom, always. Glad you asked for the help."

M–"That is still amazing to me."

K–"It's what I am guided to do and I want to. It's the least I can do."

M–"I am honored my dear. I just don't want to keep you from your soul's journey. I feel blessed already that you can come through and we can really hear each other."

K–"Me too and I am also grateful."

M–"Do you like the vibe here, south of San Felipe?"

K–"There is a quietness there that's good for you and on many levels it's very good for your healing."

M–"I will go for a little walk later. We still miss having a place in Baja. L. A. Bay was so special. Guide us to a place down here if it is for our highest and best good."

K–"Only."

M–"Love you. Talk to you later."

April 20, 2016

CHOOSING TO GO

I opened a new page on my meditation journal and began writing, "May all the Love support me. Thank You."

After I centered myself with the Infinity breath process, Kevin began…

K–"Hey Mamma."

M–"Hi honey. There is so much going on with my friend Sharon preparing to leave her body. I think you have been helping, right?"

K–"Sorry I didn't get to know her, but she's lucky to have you as a friend, Mom."

M–"Thanks honey. I am hoping you can help and greet her on your side?"

LOVE NEVER DIES

K–"I am seeing her soul and she is all Love. I will be there with all her family. Show her my pictures so she'll recognize me. She worries a bit about it all. Tell her nothing is important but her peace. She should allow all the Love in now, be in gratitude and feel it deeply. It will make her journey a celebration of her life and will set her free to so much more… Share this with her and take care of yourself. Your Angels are with you to be a loving support. You are the spiritual medium between the dimensions of Earth and Spirit. It is just who you are. Angels guide you and I am also there. I am so glad you are my mom and that we are connected for all time."

M–"Thank you, Kevin. I am honored you are my son and that you are here to help and support not only our family but our friends as well. What an amazing connection this all is. I love you."

K–"Love you too."

HELPING A FRIEND TRANSITION TO THE OTHER SIDE

I was deeply honored to be part of my friend Sharon's conscious choice to end her life. I very comforted knowing that Kevin was helping from the other side.

My dear friend Sharon Trivette had insisted to go with us to San Felipe for a week. She was a traveler at heart and had been to many places around the planet. Sharon was a single woman adventurer, and she always trusted her travels would expand her perspectives of life.

Sharon and I met a couple of years before while boarding a sailboat. Our friends Steve and Brenda White introduced me as "Janice is the *Angel Lady;* she is also a Healing Facilitator and does massage work." "Oh," Sharon replied, "I am a massage therapist. We should do a trade."

Over the following two years, we became neighbors, exchanged massage sessions, and shared many dinners at each other's homes. She and Bryan had a very fun connection, and it was always a joy to watch their interactions. This grew into wonderful love and appreciation for each other, yet that was a short-lived gift.

Sharon had been to many doctors and endured numerous tests while trying to find out why she would go into coughing and gagging episodes. She was also going to a speech therapist as she was losing the ability to enunciate her words. She knew how to slow down and breathe but couldn't stop the recurring episodes that were wearing her out. She took a leave of absence from work to rest up and see if that might help.

I was not sure if she was up for a road trip to San Felipe, but she insisted, so off we went as a threesome. We eventually made it to our friend's home south of the border, engine troubles and all. The third morning, Bryan and I decided to tip toe out of the guest house and take a quad ride down the beach. When we returned, we found Sharon still asleep. She was normally an early riser, so something felt wrong to me. I walked over to her bed and softly said, "Hey girl, you going to sleep all day?" There was no response or movement at all. I gently shook her shoulder and said in a louder voice, "Sharon, Sharon, wake up." As I turned her body, her eyes rolled, but there was no response. I quickly checked for a pulse and found it to be very weak.

I shouted out to Bryan, "We need an ambulance now!" Thank goodness a great volunteer medical response team swiftly appear out of nowhere. As the emergency crew showed up, I knew I should pack a bag and ride with her. We ended up at a little clinic in town where she was given more oxygen, which helped her come back to consciousness. I talked with the doctor through a computer to translate what he was saying in Spanish. It was clear that she immediately needed to return in the U.S. and get to the nearest hospital.

LOVE NEVER DIES

It was a long and crazy ride. I prayed all the way. "Hang in there Sharon. I love you. We're going to get the help you need. God is right where you are." We finally made it back to a hospital near our home in Encinitas, California.

I called a good friend of Sharon's, a doctor who lived in Maui, and, interestingly enough, she believed the doctors had not diagnosed Sharon properly. She felt that our friend might have amyotrophic lateral sclerosis (ALS), also known as Lou Gehrig's disease. With more testing, it turned out to confirm this sad diagnostic for this progressive chronic disease of the motor neurons which affects the electrical stimulation to all parts of the body.

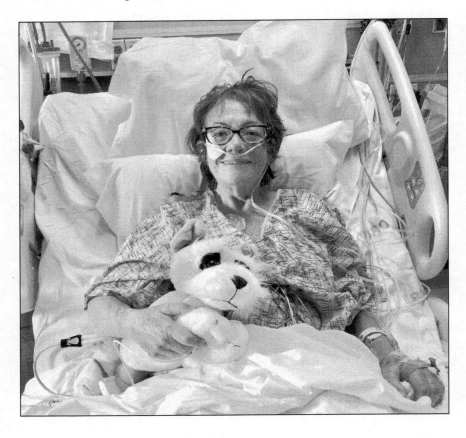

Sharon was now clearly conscious that the oxygen levels were maintained for her. She had seen too many other people suffer through this debilitating and fatal disease at La Costa Glen, a senior retirement center where she worked as a massage therapist. A week later, Sharon left the hospital for a nursing home. After a few weeks, arrangements were made so she could go to her place with hospice in-home help.

The new "Death with Dignity Act" had just been passed in California. It provided patients with the right to end their life if there was a fatal diagnosis for six months or less. Sharon immediately chose that path and with help, put her life collections in order. She took care of business and was ready to go. There was nothing wrong with her ability to think clearly. It seemed strange to all her friends and family, but we honored her right to choose and helped in any way we could.

I was truly honored to be asked to be with her when she left this earth on April 21st. As she lay on a bed, I sat by her side and held her hand. A friend cradled her head while another one was at her feet. The doctor administered the lethal doses of medications, and Sharon felt no discomfort. She looked me deeply in the eyes and I said, "Go with the Angels, they are all around you now. Just let go my dear… Let go." She closed her eyes and within a few minutes I could feel her spirit leave her body. I then heard her say, "Wow, this is great!" and off she went. An amazing experience of Love that I will never forget.

Chapter 7

Awakening Here or There

"Many people are suffering deep emotional anguish beneath the surface of their lives, and smile even as they hurt inside."
—Jim Palmer

There is a new awakening available when you have courage to feel. It is not easy, but it is the only way through. Avoiding your feelings only increases their intensity. Kevin realized this too late. As a mom, I can't go around my deep hurts and pains either. I am learning a whole new level of trusting life with all its ups and downs. I can be awake enough to open up to the amazing ways Love shows up.

April 27, 2016

SELF-FORGIVENESS

After my breathing and meditating, I realized that I had a question for Kevin...

M–"How are you doing with self-forgiveness?"

K–"I guess forgiveness is part of why I choose to be or even why I can be with you. Being with you is not because I'm feeling guilty. It's coming from a place in me that wants to be there for you. You really have forgiven me for the awful memory that I shot myself. The mental picture you have of me lying on that hospital bed must be horrifying. I feel like I owe you. It's the least I can do! I am just glad that I can be there and that you are open to *hearing* me."

M–"It's an image I wish I could get out of my memory forever. I am just so sorry that you saw no other way to deal with the situation. I would have done *anything* to help if you had let me."

K–"I know, Mom. I know, but it was my mess! I felt stuck in my job and in my relationship. I loved my girlfriend, but I couldn't continue to live in that situation. I feared that she might have ended her own life if I had left her. My guilt and the potential feeling of being responsible for her death were too much to handle. At that time, I made her life more important than mine. I have shared before how my life was even more complicated than that. I was feeling so defeated in my mortgage job. I continued lying about going to work, although I had quit weeks before. It just added up and built a *huge mess* inside of me."

M–"I understand, Kevin, but *your life* mattered."

K–"Right, well too late now. Here I am."

M–"I can feel the sadness and desperation that you experienced. I know it took courage to end your life yet staying would have required even more. It is really beyond me, and it just makes me cry. This really is the worst thing a mother could feel, losing her baby…a son who brought his smile and lightness to so many…loved by so many, and missed by all!"

K–"I know, Mom. I am so sorry, but maybe through us both, we can help others."

M–"Maybe, but I want to know from your side now. *Do you see if there might have been another way?* I mean, what good can we do if you are saying that when things get hard, in a relationship or in life, you just give up and kill yourself? Damn! I was married four times before I met Bryan. I often felt that I was lost. I was terrified each time I had to leave a relationship or tell the truth about how it wasn't working. I *still* had to change and somehow learn to *TRUST in the unknown."*

K–"Well that's it, Mom, that's it right there. *I didn't trust.* I didn't have the faith and here I am. I was praying hard to God and my Angels for forgiveness and help, but I didn't trust that I was deserving of their help. I will be working on this self-forgiveness for a while. I just feel so bad for hurting you and so many others, like my girlfriend who has gone through so much pain because of the way I left."

M–"*I know God is right where you are.* Your soul is moving into the knowingness that *Love is who you are and who you will always be.* Learn from the limitations you felt, saw, sensed, and *know that you are divine,* and I really mean it. You are a *Divine Creation* and miracle of God. I will *always* be grateful for our short time together here on Earth. I just want you to find your peace and express the Love and deep joy of your uniqueness."

"I know that my work, *my choice,* is to move through this sadness and all the tears and to trust at an even deeper level. I see you in the hands of God being loved unconditionally for eternity."

K–"Yes Mom, we are all on that journey of awakening, there or here. We are all meant to be and express that Love. *Trust in that Love.* So, Mom, *you must trust that right now!* I see your courage to feel. Your strength is in knowing this Truth and keeping the faith that we are never alone on our journey, which never ends. Love is never ending and the more you can feel that, while you are still in a body, the better. *Life is about allowing the feelings IN your body."*

"There is only One Power and Presence of Love and being in a body is a gift we are given! We can awaken through all our suffering, that's the good news. There is always Love and support for continued expansion as a soul. It is always our choice. There are just levels of awareness and awakening…"

"Love your life, Mom, and remind others to love theirs, even with the hurts, pains, and difficulties along the way. Feel through it, while looking for the beauty. It's all around. My love is with you. I am so glad you are my mom. I will love you forever. *TRUST, Mom, TRUST. Trust* through the tears, for your heart is breaking open to be all you were meant to be."

M–"Thank you, Kevin. Until the next time we talk, I will *trust* more deeply that Love is with you and me. I believe it's what we truly are."

June 25, 2016

STRONG AND CLEAR CONFIRMATION

I have gone through two painful foot surgeries in the last nine months. It was now time to hit the road for an adventure to the Four Corners area. Our trip was just what I needed to get a new perspective on life.

Our journey took us through Sedona, where we spent five days with our friends Jill and Michael. We went up to the Grand Canyon and through the beauty and the green of Colorado. Then we drove south into New Mexico and spent three wonderful days in Ojo Caliente, a sacred healing site of hot springs used by native Indians for centuries. This is where I experienced an amazing healing with my ankle. On the last day, I was surprised to feel the swelling and pain completely fade away.

Right before we took off, as we were getting the camper ready. Bryan was outside, so I decided to be bold and just speak to Kevin out loud. "Kevin, I want you to show me that you are with me. Give me a sign so clear that I won't have one little doubt about it. Make it so outrageous that I really can't miss it! I know I'm asking a lot, but hey, anything's possible, so go for it." I kind of smirked and smiled at myself, thinking, "You're a silly girl!" and I really meant it.

We got on the road and continued our journey. As we drove along the Rio Grande towards Taos, I needed to take a break from sitting and the dog needed to be walked. I suggested to Bryan to get off at the upcoming Ranger station.

We ended up taking a longer stop than we had expected. Bryan got into a discussion with a very talkative Ranger about the area. It was a bit more information than we needed to know, I thought at the time.

As we walked back through the parking lot, we noticed that it was now full of cars and buses everywhere. Suddenly, I heard, "Janice, Janice!" I wondered, "What? Is somebody calling me?" And I heard again, "Janice!" from a woman running towards me with her arms wide open. I recognized her from Idyllwild but couldn't remember her name in that moment. She gave me a great big hug while asking, "How are you doing?"

I was so surprised and replied, "Oh my gosh, I haven't seen you since Kevin's memorial." I explained that we were having our first big outing and I was doing well. She was warm, friendly, a truly caring and loving person. Her two daughters were Kevin's friends from school. I was wondering why she was in the area. "What are you doing way out here?", I asked her. She explained that she was with her girls, waiting in line behind a bus, ready to leave for a white-water rafting trip. "Oh, that is so cool!" I replied. Her daughters ran across the parking lot towards us. We hugged, chatted a bit, and cried together as we all missed Kevin. It was a very heartfelt and sweet moment, a thousand miles away from Idyllwild!

I wished them all an amazing trip and they left, blowing kisses as we waved goodbye. Bryan and I got in the car bewildered and I was stunned from this surprise encounter. As we started to drive out of the parking lot, it dawned on me; it had to be Kevin bringing this together. I said out loud, "Oh my God Kevin, I get it! How did you do that?" It was so amazing and so clear to me that Kevin had worked every angle to bring us into this parking lot at the perfect time for us to see each other. Even the extended chat with the Ranger was timed perfectly for the encounter to happen. So, I got it. I knew that Kevin was truly with me at that moment, and he had heard my request loud and clear. It was such a strong confirmation that could not be denied!

June 30, 2016

KNOW THAT YOU ARE LOVED

It has been 9 months since Kevin's Memorial. I came back up the hill on the mountain top of Idyllwild, California, where I had lived for 25 years. I wanted to visit my friends and personally thank some of them for all the work and love they put into bringing all the details together for the Memorial. I was honored to be asked by my dear friend Hollis Fulmor to lead a meditation group that evening at Spirit Mountain Retreat.

Sitting in a circle, I began with an opening prayer and then shared briefly about my communications with Kevin. "Earlier today, I meditated and asked for guidance. I will now share with you those words we had together."

"Consciously open to your guidance; it is always waiting for you. Life is a journey in a physical body, and we have a vast array of choices about what to do with our time while we are here. It is a gift we have been given, the gift of being in this miraculous body and living on this beautiful planet. We have choices around what to do with our time or where to focus our attention. The moment we don't seem to have choice is when we move into reaction. How do we feel what is pushing us, from the inside? It is by observing our reactions that we can understand our level of awareness. What is really working in alignment to our happiness? What feels good and what does not? Are we choosing to observe and look for Love, or are we reacting and coming from fear and lack in some way?"

"*Looking from Love, we find the compass to compassion* for ourselves and others. If we look from judgment, we separate ourselves."

"When we learn to go within and let go of the 'doingness' and 'busyness' of life, we come to the core of the Love that we are. This unique expression is our gift, not only to life, but also to all of creation."

"If we think that we are separate and alone, we have not remembered the continuous source of Love that created us. We will also miss the many expressions of Love with us in the unseen realms. It is about our *awakening and our willingness* to open our minds and hearts to feel, sense and *know our Oneness*. This is an ongoing process, one that will continually amaze and guide us."

"Are we willing to let go of the illusion of being in control? Take time to breathe in a conscious way and not be run by the mind. Learn to be aware from a higher place. This is where we find the guidance, peace, and love to then move out in our world. When life gets hard and we are challenged, can we find an inner peace? Can we still believe in Love? Can we remember that we are not alone? Can we feel that inside? *Can we even trust in the face of death?"*

Chapter 8

Don't Give Up

"When our days become dreary with low-hovering clouds of despair, and when our nights become darker than a thousand midnights, let us remember that there is a creative force in this universe, working to pull down the gigantic mountains of evil, a power that is able to make a way out of no way, and transform dark yesterdays into bright tomorrows."
—Martin Luther King Jr.

Forgiveness is such an essential part of healing. To not only forgive others but to forgive ourselves. You must dig deep into your heart and keep letting go. It is a process, but we can get there. The lesson is to not give up!

August 9, 2016

THE LESSON

M–"So, what are you doing on the other side?"

K–"Feeling the peace. It is so good to feel that, and really let it in. I was really torn with what seemed to be *darkness with no hope*, no way out, and the feeling that I couldn't do it all. I was feeling so wrong that I couldn't figure it out and if I couldn't, there had to be something wrong with me. It was all too much! Too much for me to figure out on my own and I was not trusting any help."

M–"Do you think that if you had asked for help it would have changed things?"

LOVE NEVER DIES

K–"*No!* Because I believed that my girlfriend might kill herself if I left her!"

M–"Well, let's get this right, Kevin. You did the ending, and she is still alive! Right?"

K–"*OK, right,* but I couldn't live with that possibility. So, I left, and that's my bottom line!"

M–"Yep! I hear that, but people say things they don't mean when they feel desperate. The saddest thing is you couldn't live with that possibility or that sense of responsibility. I get it, but it sucks in many ways, and I miss you!"

K–"I know, Mom, but would you rather see me here, finding peace, or there, feeling so damn stuck?"

M–"I guess I will always imagine other scenarios. I feel there could have been many people and professionals able to help; things like couples and personal counseling… You might have seen what wasn't working and been able to move forward with a better understanding about yourself. But without help, you only found the drastic answer of ending your life."

K–"*I GET IT, MOM. I DO!* But I didn't see that before. *Maybe there was hope and I gave up too soon! MY LESSON!*"

M–"*THE LESSON… NOT TO GIVE UP?*"

K–"*Not to run away! My karma, my lesson.*"

M–"Yes, my Dear, and I love you no less for it."

K–"Well, Mom, that is right where we started this conversation… I am feeling more peace and I know that I will learn a lot more now. I am where I am, and I am OK with it. I know you miss me, and I know I hurt you, *but I'M NOT DEAD."*

"Mom, be happy that we will always be connected by our Love. It really is the bond through time which lessens the pain, with the Grace and Peace that God has given us. In that realization, there is the Joy that *LOVE LIVES ON.* I love you, Mom, with all my heart. I am so grateful that you are courageous enough to feel the pain and joy of Love and *NOT* run away from it. You show me how I could have been and what to strive for *if* I get a chance to come back into a human form again. *The courage to Love again!* You have it Mom, and I love you so much."

M–"I Love you too, Kevin."

After this exchange I cried like I was never going to stop. It was such as deep process to listen and write what he was saying, yet at the same time, trying to understand his perspective.

The sound of our grandchildren playing in the forest pulled my awareness back to this reality. As I looked in their direction, I observed the sweetness and innocence of laughter and felt the joy. It reminded me how blessed I was to have an extended family with Bryan. The children were having so much fun! I wish Kevin could be with us physically to experience them all…yet I knew his awareness was actually there and that made me very happy.

September 14, 2016

BE WILLING TO FEEL!

M–"God Morning Christ, my Angels, Guides, and my Kevin in Heaven!"

I immediately heard, "You are perfect just the way you are." *If* that is true, there should be no problem within me. Right? Help me see from this place of fullness and peace. Help me hear your guidance clearly.

I heard the words and began to write…

"To be perfect means you are whole. Nothing is missing within you. You are whole from the Love that created you. A Divine expression of everything it took in the Universe to bring you to this place as the Energy that you are. *Everything you need has been given for you to be, learn and give, and there is so much more beyond what is seen.* Every cell of the 'physical you' and your Soul *express your essen*ce and continually supports you being here."

"Everything is provided!" The air to breathe, the water to keep you 'fluid,' the food that nurtures your body, eyes to see the beauty of the sunrise and amazing sunsets, and ears to hear the hum of life happening around you, even to the smallest chirp of hummingbirds outside your window. Just feel into this moment. What is here? Become present and go within to the tight places. Just allow them to be."

"Are you brave enough to feel the holding? Can you see from a Higher Perspective?"

"I must be willing to feel the knot in my gut," I said to myself. I then took a deep breath and continued to listen.

"To see the beauty and feel the expansion, you must also feel the discomfort. Looking deeper within takes courage, Janice, and *you* have this. You can go through the discomfort to listen, feel, and see beyond, from a place of peace and connectedness to so much more."

"When you surrender the struggling thoughts that you are somehow not enough or the belief that you need to be more, then it is from that place that you receive guidance. Your true expression comes from this place of surrendering and stillness, which is the wisdom you sense and feel right now. A shift occurs when you finally let go of trying to control what is happening in your physical world and remember that your struggles are here to assist you in finding yourself within. Once you surrender, you have the ability to experience yourself as wholeness.

This will be in perfect alignment with what you are created from and who you really are. That blessing is the gift God has given you."

"Be solid in the Love that created you and that you are. All is well. Be at Peace."

September 22, 2016

AWAKEN FROM THE PAST!

M–"God Day! Thanks for the rain. I am thankful for Bryan who is willing to come to counseling with me. It is helping me to clear old pains of helplessness, frustration, and abandonment from my past. *I want to let it all go* so I can be free to Love others and myself, without conditions. There are many people around me suffering. This is leading to my own frustrations and pain, especially when I perceived that they are not loving themselves enough to receive the Love I have to give. I had initially felt the deep helplessness of not be able to help others as a child. Counseling helped me realize that the unhappiness of others was never my responsibility to fix. It's a lot to process, but at least I am now seeing it clearly and I know what dragon I am facing."

"Help me, Dear God, to see clearly and help me love myself and others unconditionally. What more do I need to see or clear? Thank You for all your support, wisdom, and Love. I will now breathe and listen."

Then, I heard the words and began to write…

"Your ability to care so deeply is your Love. When you connect to human suffering and pain related to what someone does (or does not do), you take it personally. Yet, they are not purposely doing anything to you. Let us look at your father…"

"It was not that he did not love you if he was not present for you emotionally. He was lost in his own suffering. It was his own world of learning to love and find himself, yet to you, he appeared quite lost in his own process. This was never meant for you to figure out and most certainly not yours to fix. It was your father's personal journey of realization."

"No matter what has, or has not, happened, what was said or never said at all, it was only about him, really. The thoughts you formed around his treatment of you and the resulting emotions that you felt are about you. That is now part of your journey to self-realization. The experience of watching your father's anger and abusive actions toward your brother and mother also impacted you deeply. Even those feelings will one day be released and be healed through your surrendering."

"Can you imagine your father, as a child, being buggy whipped in front of townspeople by his own father? Is there anything he could have done as an innocent child to deserve this? *No!* It was not about your father. It was about your grandfather's frustration, anger and mistreatment from his father now acted out unconsciously on his own son."

"You are here to see the goodness in others, even when they cannot see or feel it themselves. You are here to awaken from the past, which is being acted out, generation after generation, from battles that are now in the past."

"Is it now time to put down the swords of anger and find your Peace within? When the suffering, anger, hate, and resentment become unbearable to hold, then one falls to their knees in exhaustion from the battle within. That's when an opportunity for healing can happen."

"Nelson Mandela forgave his jailers. The apartheid of white supremacy and dominance over people of different ethnicity was a heavy cross to bear. Yet, because Love opened his heart to awaken, he was able to forgive his jailers. He also had Divine Guidance and support to do the work needed to bring Peace to the country."

"There are no accidents. You recently watched the movie about his life, Janice. You have been given eternity to awaken. It is about allowing Compassion and Forgiveness within. To see where the past pains are held inside you and to release them by forgiving all, Jesus said, 'Forgive them all, as they know not what they do.'"

"So, forgive them all, Janice. Your father, brother and all the men that would only love you to the degree in which they could love. All of them are on their own path of awakening, and you are also moving on your own journey. Just love them all unconditionally, which is without holding back your full Love. It is also about *learning to love yourself unconditionally.* Let Love shine brightly in all directions from your heart, beyond what words can reach. Be the Love that you are and be here to express and share your journey. You shine for others to see."

M–"Thank You! Who is it that speaks?" I then heard, "God, Christ, the voice of Wisdom and Truth that is within… Be at Peace."

Wow! The Wisdom within me, I thought, God, which is everywhere and in everything. The voice of Wisdom is always waiting here for me, but somehow in that moment it was much clearer than ever before. I felt like I was in a deeper Peace than I had ever experienced. I almost didn't want to move from this deep place of receptivity, but I have sat for hours here in my chair and my legs needed to move. My back felt compressed, and my rear end was almost numb. Yes, it was time to move out into my life and integrate this awakening. THANK YOU, GOD!

I would like to speak about the importance of healthy boundaries. I don't want anyone to think that Love is about putting up with verbal or physical abuse in any way. As we grow in our awareness, we learn to feel what Love is and what it is not. We feel and see the difference between what is forwarding and comes from the heart and what behaviors and words diminish our Soul.

The question to ask is, "What am I learning and how am I feeling right now?" Are you willing to ask yourself, "Is this working for me? Can I thrive in this relationship?" It is important to realize that you cannot make someone else Love you the way that you believe it should feel. Either you are both open to learning what loving feels like between each other and are willing to make conscious changes that honor each other, or you don't. It always comes back to you. Ask yourself, "What do I need to do to show up and Love myself?" This is not selfish. This is where Love starts…with you. Learn to Love yourself and you will know what to embrace and what to release.

Dear Human,
You've got it all wrong.
You didn't come here to master unconditional love.
This is where you came from and where you'll return.

You came here to learn personal love.
Universal love.
Messy love.
Sweaty Love.
Crazy love.
Broken love.
Whole love.
Infused with divinity.
Lived through the grace of stumbling
Demonstrated through the beauty of… messing up.
Often.

You didn't come here to be perfect, you already are.
You came here to be gorgeously human. Flawed and fabulous.
And rising again into remembering.
But unconditional love? Stop telling that story.
Love in truth doesn't need any adjectives.
It doesn't require modifiers.
It doesn't require the condition of perfection.

It only asks you to show up.
And do your best.
That you stay present and feel fully
That you shine and fly and laugh and cry and hurt and heal and fall
and get back up and play and
work and live and die as you.
It's enough.
It's plenty.

—C. Walsh

Chapter 9

Do Good in the World

"You have incarnated so you may feel love and joy. Allow yourself to feel without judgment, as even the warrior needs to cry."
—Christian Sørensen

Deep reflection offers the ability to look back and see if there could have been a better way to handle or react to a situation in our life. Learning to have compassion for ourselves and each other is the way to grow beyond our past and experience a better and more positive now.

September 24, 2016

It's been one year to the day that Kevin took his own life.

THE PAIN/THE LEARNING

M–"I am open to God, Christ, my Angels, and my Kevin in Heaven. May your loving guidance speak to me now, and our family."

"I love you so much my Dear Kevin and I have learned a lot in this past year about the illusion of death and truth. Thank you for being with me and sharing some insights. Thank you for letting me know that you are still with me and that you're not really dead. You're just without a physical body. Thank you for teaching me about the *'GOD GLUE'* and for explaining that through true forgiveness and deep Love we can still connect."

"I know you have been silent in the past weeks while I have been going even deeper into finding my freedom by letting go of loving conditionally. I am healing an unconscious pain that my little self has carried around from my relationship to my father. I have also learned more about moving on from relationships because of the pain I had to face with your abrupt passing. I cannot change or rescue anyone when I see their suffering or their inability to move through it. The truth is, when I saw others in pain, it was unconsciously triggering my own unknown pain within. I was feeling better equipped to tell others how to heal their situations, yet ill-equipped to feel and heal my own suffering. This really is about all of us learning to love and heal within."

"It is an inside job to feel your pain and to build the courage to experience it fully. When your heart feels broken, bringing love, understanding and forgiveness to the pain allows *GRACE to* enter. When I hold a deeper understanding, with compassion and without judgment, I find that I walk closer to Christ. I carry a pure stand for Love and forgiveness. There is a much deeper awareness that we are *all* on this journey to finding our strength and feeling this Oneness. **Right now** is the most important moment we have on this journey that never ends. Thank you, Kevin, for helping me to get it. Thank you for hearing me. I know you do… I love you. Is there something *you* would like to share now?"

K–"Love you too, Mommy, Mom, Mother. I know it is silly that I still like to call you Mommy, but you then know the Love and sweetness that I feel towards you when I do."

M–"Yes, and it's just fine."

K–"Good, I know you miss me and wish I could be seen by all, but I am with you, Chad, Arie, Dad, my girlfriend and many more that miss me. Remember, I experience a multidimensional reality."

"I am sorry for my actions that have caused such pain. I see how each of you has processed *or* refused to process that pain. My pain is mine and yours is yours to deal with now. It sucks, but ultimately you must learn what is yours to change, and why you are reacting the way you are. Yes, Mom, *it takes courage,* and I am so proud to see you face your fears and do whatever it takes to move through them. I am glad that you are finding your strength, your voice and I know you will help many with this. Just one step at a time, Mom. I am by your side. I also have much to learn."

"*I am learning about Love and having Compassion for myself,* which is the hardest, before loving all others. It's about being patient, kind and, no matter what, *Trusting* that we are given the *Gift of life*. I am sorry that I did not know what else to do, but to end it. I do miss you all and I cannot change what I have done. Just learn and do good in the world. Be a part of the Joy and truth that each of us are. I didn't get it there and there is still more learning for me to do. I hope God gives me the chance to come back again so I can do it differently; make a positive impact and not create pain."

"*I am sorry.*"

"*I Love You All!*"

"*I am with you.*"

"Thank you for Loving me and knowing me as Love and Joy. God Bless Us All."

M–"And so it is, my Dear One, and so it is."

Oct. 5, 2016

LEAVE A HAPPIER VIBE

Twenty-six years ago today, I gave birth to a beautiful little boy, my Kevin, now in Heaven for a year. It was an honor and a joy to bring him into this world. He was JOY. **So, my Sweet one, Happy Birthday**. I wonder what you are feeling and your thoughts on this day. I will now breathe and let go…

LOVE NEVER DIES

M–"I love you Kevin."

K–"I Love you too, Momma. That's a deep question, Mom. I wish I could physically be celebrating with you all. From this place of Oneness and observation, I feel you all. I feel you Momma, the one that gave me birth. I feel you missing me but *do not be sad*. There has been enough of that in this last year. I can only say that I miss you and I am with you."

"To be in an expanded place of awareness is amazing and the ability to be multidimensional is far out. At the same time, I am not removed from what I did and the effect it has had on so many. I want to come back, be stronger and leave a stronger, happier vibe behind. I want to learn to have patience and Love myself and have deep compassion and Love for others. It's not like I am judged by anything or anyone. It's just the Love that I am, the goodness that I am, that wants to make a difference."

"We all play different roles for each other while learning to love, forgive and evolve. I played out roles in my lifetime… The wave of that is so much bigger than I could have ever known. I continue to see and learn from it. MY LOVE IS BIGGER THAN THE EXPANDING UNIVERSE, MOM! LOVE YOU FOREVER AND ALWAYS! PEACE AND LOVE TO ALL."

Kevin is the one who gave me a birthday gift that day and I love sharing his words.

Dec. 2, 2016

SUFFERING CAN AWAKEN US BACK TO LOVE

M–"God Day! I observe, feel, and know this is a God Day as I pause into the stillness. I breathe in the peace that melts down through me… I breathe out and let it go… I watch my thoughts and know I am not that. The stillness brings me back. The softness expands with every breath… As I release the breath with ease, I am surrendered into this Peace. My awareness expands to the Light around and within me. My thoughts are like a butterfly coming back to rest on the flower of peace; resting and breathing as wings are opening and closing. I am feeling the warmth of the Golden Rays… I am surrendered to this Peace and Love now…"

M–"Now, my Kevin in heaven, are you with me? I Love You!"

K–"I Love you too, Momma, I see and feel your pain regarding Grandma and Gordon. You're wanting to make a difference, yet they have chosen the path they are on. It is their dynamics, their suffering, their pain. Keep uncovering your own pain, there's more. When you've healed and cleared those childhood wounds, then observing your mother and brother will bring you feelings of compassion and less pain."

"It is no accident that you had a client coming to see you yesterday and you were guided to show her how her parent's pains and sufferings were not hers. As children, you both felt the deep unhappiness around and you wanted to make a difference with everything from deep within your hearts. I felt the same way with you and Dad."

M–"The weight is too much to carry. It is a knot inside that we must untie. This is done with understanding and forgiveness. Doing the prayer 'Of Forgiveness' is a good way of connecting to the Love for each other and taking responsibility for the part we have played. By calling in the other person energetically, we are calling in their Higher Self and taking responsibility for any judgment or part we have played in the situation."

I am so sorry.
Please forgive me.
Thank you.
I love you.

"Know that this Ho'oponopono prayer is heard at the deepest level, as it peels off the layers of the hurt and pain we can carry."

K–"Yes, Mom. I Love you. I am so sorry. Please forgive me. Thank you."

M–"Yes, I see there truly is just Compassion and Love. Nothing to hang on to, just pure tears of Compassion and Pure Love."

K–"Yes Mom, we feel because we care. As much as you have always wanted me free of my suffering, it has served a purpose. It awakened me back to Love. The deeper intelligence of our heart knows that it is real. You know who you are, Mom, it is *Love. Just be that* and radiate it, as I know you always do. That is *true* freedom.

M–"You have become *wiser,* my Dear."

K–"I am learning by watching you. Don't get stuck on someone else's suffering. Remember, you will only get stuck if your unconscious pain reflects that which you perceive in others. To feel is to be real.

Compassion, understanding without judgment, is true freedom. This is the gift of God within us all…this opens Infinity and the expansion which we are all part of."

M–"Wow! I cannot fully express how honored I am to be connected with you. I know you are in a place of Wisdom and Love. Thank You my Kevin in Heaven. May you continue to grow and expand in the most wonderful of ways. I love you as big as the expanding Universe!"

K–"Happy to expand you, Mom, I love you too! *It's OK to be HAPPY.*"

January 23, 2016

OPERATING UNDER A CLOUD

M–"Am I feeling you, Kevin?"

K–"Yes, Mamma, I am here."

M–"Am I hearing you? It's a little fuzzy hearing you and I don't want to ever make this connection up."

K–"Just want it to *be real,* Mom?"

M–"Right."

K–"It's real and I am here. Sorry you have been sick and dealing with a lot that can weigh you down. Glad Bryan is good. I was watching the doctor going into his heart. He's a good doctor. Bryan is doing better now, and you are not to worry."

M–"OK, I sure see how worrying doesn't work. I have learned this from watching Grandma always being in fear for the smallest of things. It feels like a disease of the mind... From your perspective, does every thought we have really matter, Kevin?"

K–"Big question, Mom, but *it does matter* because it can build up a pattern of energy which becomes a belief."

M–"Like a storm?"

K–"Well, thoughts are gathering and building for sure. Can't even say if it's positive or negative, but each thought with the same energy gathers more of itself and forms the structure of a belief."

M–"Whether it's really true or not?"

K–"Right. We are the creators with our perceptions of reality."

M–"That's pretty powerful. I've never quite got it so straight forwardly as that. *I am the creator* and I create from believing in... It's one's beliefs about literally everything that forms their perceptions of reality.

K–"Right."

M–"So, anything can become real for a person? Seems like one's beliefs are what moves them throughout their life, even if the beliefs are not based on truth."

K–"Only if they keep believing them."

M–"Right."

K–"But...just because you have a belief, that doesn't make it fixed, even if you've been believing it for a very long time or if you have held it for lifetimes. It's up to each person to be what they choose. One can expand or contract whatever they choose and that is the *free will* given to each Soul carrying a physical body."

M–"You have gotten pretty wise, my Dear. Easier to see from Spirit? You are *Science of Mind 101*."

K–"Well, this is what you were trying to teach me and what you are still learning yourself."

M–"For sure. It's like you can get lost in your own haze of beliefs and not even realize you're doing it."

K–"It's not over yet, Mom and you just need to get clear and keep moving forward with what you want. If you knew all the support from the Universe that is being supplied to you as you reach out, you would be aware of the hands of Love that reach back to help you. You get the idea? You know that who you are is making a difference, Mom. The lie you have been believing is, 'What I do or what I know doesn't make a difference.' You began to believe this when you were a little girl."

M–"When I felt powerless to help my Mother and Father?"

K–"Yes. So, do you do get it, Mom? You have been under that old cloud from your mom's limitations. You get down when you start feeling helpless. Know who you are, *'The Angel Lady.'* Remember this from your own *real* experiences. I want to you to remember when you reached into the bag at the dump truck with the Angel gifts. You always stand in the Light of Love with your Angels, working with them to help other people. This *IS* who you are, and I am proud to be your son. Don't get caught up in other people's drama. Like you just told Grandma in the hospital today, 'God is right where you are.' Just hold the *high watch*, Mom. Knowing the Love that we are and which we are created from, is more real than any dramas and limitations we can create. *Too bad I didn't get that."*

M–"You can say that *now*. At least you get it and you can remind me when I forget. Thank you, Kevin, for coming through. I am so proud of you and your growing wisdom. Love you as big as the expanding Universe."

K–"Write your books, Mom. Paint the beauty. Share the Infinity Love Process. Who you are does make a difference."

> *"Hope, smiles from the threshold of the year to come, whispering, 'It will be happier.'"*
> —Alfred Tennyson

Chapter 10

The Santa Claus Gift

"Even when we are in the thick muddiness of our pain, despair, and tenderness, we can grow through it as long as we are alive and present enough to bear witness."
— Alex Elle

March 2, 2017

My husband declared, "It is time for you to get out these four walls! A road trip is just what you need." I am 66 and I haven't felt in my prime lately. This is mostly due to being bed ridden for many months. My ankle had no ligaments to hold my foot to my lower leg; therefore, I needed two painful surgeries. That situation slowed me way down, along with my metabolism! Without revealing numbers, let's just say I have gained some weight, but my 6'2" eyes of blue, still finds me fetching…it's all good!

THE BAJA JOURNEY

Bryan, my amazing husband, knew exactly what I needed. It was time to for a camping adventure, back in nature. We had wanted to do this trip for a long time, and I think we were ready to drive pass the turn-off for Bahia de Los Angeles with open gratitude and sadness. We once had a large geodesic dome that Bryan had built in the Bay of Angels. Life moved us out of there, kicking and screaming. It was a piece of heaven, and we deeply missed our home there. It has taken some time, but we were now ready to have a new adventure. As we shared our beautiful memories with each other, I also added aloud, "Angels and my Kevin in Heaven, please guide us on this journey to an even better home, if it is for our Highest and Best Good!"

We drove down the Baja Peninsula and camped seven nights before reaching Conception Bay. I asked Bryan if we could find somewhere for dinner and a place to stay the night as we still had not figured out where we would set up camp in the area. Bryan knew the perfect place, just south of Mulegé. He discovered the area years before when he had a plane and flew to the Hotel Serenidad airstrip.

We pulled in and parked right next to a truck and trailer. A man looking exactly like Santa Claus shouted out with a happy, "Top of the evening to you, where are you headed?" He asked with great gusto. "Well, we don't really know, but somewhere in Conception Bay," Bryan replied. "How about you?" Bryan asked. "Well, I have been camped for the last few months in the best place, Coyote Bay, but as I started down the road, my indicator lights came on, so I thought I best have them checked out before I got too far out of town." He then went on to tell us how to find his perfect spot on the bay. I was delighted as this was a perfect timing for 'Santa Claus' to be there and explain how to find this new campsite. I knew it was a gift and realized Kevin and our Angels were working overtime to bring that together!

We found a beautiful campsite in Coyote Bay, right on the ocean. It is so gorgeous, even if a bit windy. I am, however, so happy to be sitting on the beach with my toes in the sand looking out upon the blues, aquas and greens swirling in the Sea of Cortez. It is more peaceful here than the Pacific side of Baja. We are surrounded by the brown rolling sand hills dotted sparsely with green cacti. The mountaintops, cresting above the hills, give the illusion of islands splashed across the marbled blue sea. It is a truly majestic place.

Bryan is taking a well-deserved siesta since he did all the driving. It's been quite a journey, trusting our process, which is allowing our inner wisdom to guide the way. We like not having a plan when we do these camping trips. It always works out in the best way possible.

Sitting on the beach, soaking in the beauty, I find myself not only playing with Kilo, my cutest dog ever, but also balancing my notebook on one leg and writing about how good I am feeling in this moment. I am once again able to relax, read, and enjoy the splendor of nature. Life is Good and I feel myself melting into bliss.

Music has always been a big part of my life. As we drove, I often played my most treasured CD of songs that Kevin made for me when he was 17. It always brings tears to my eyes as I begin to listen and remember the joy it brought both of us. He looked up from his computer, that day, and asked me what else I would like. "I like it all Kevin," I replied. "Also, throw in some good old Beatles." He wrote "MOM'S MIX" with his black sharpie on the only CD he ever made for me. I wish I had asked for more... He had such happiness and joy creating it for me.

I will never totally understand why Kevin chose to take his own life. His experience of the sadness and pressure he felt must have been huge. He was trying to make it in this world with a new job in refinance and he was having challenges in his relationship with his girlfriend. It was shocking to everyone that he could see no other way. Over the last year, he seemed to withdraw from everyone, including me. His brother Arie, who was two and a half years older, and his half-brother Chad, 16 years older, had little or no communication with him as well. Kevin's father, John, was also frustrated with his inabilities to change the difficulties he was seeing in Kevin. It is a very hard thing to accept that no one could help him. The saying 'Pride Goeth Before the Fall,' comes to mind again. How could he hold in his fear and suffering so much that no one knew the depth of it?

I did not want another day to go by without reviewing the vivid and joyful dream I had with Kevin the night before. It has been a year and almost six months ago to the day of his passing. I didn't want to be sad in such a beautiful place but, I was there to let go and really allow myself to feel the sadness. My thoughts were returning to the joyous connection we had in my dream from the previous night. It was one of the clearest and most real interactions I had with Kevin in dream time after our flying experience.

MY DREAM WITH KEVIN

We were at a retreat center that had a large bookstore and outside were beautiful trees and green rolling lawns. It was a happy place with people interacting in peaceful and joyous ways. I was with Bryan, and he had to leave to go flying with someone. As I walked outside, Kevin was standing on the lawn with a big smile, very happy to see me. We were thrilled to be back together and feeling the joy of love we so often shared. To be with him again and to experience him was so realistic and amazing!

A woman and her daughters, who I had remembered being at Kevin's Memorial, walked up to me. She asked how I was doing, and I said, "Great, I am just so amazed he's here. Can you see him too?" "Yes, but how is that possible?" she asked. "I don't know, but there he is." By this time, we watched him playing with four teenage girls, all romping in the grass and laughing with him. What a joyous sight to see him so happy and playing again. He would glance back at me to keep the connection and smile. Kevin ran back to me and picked me up in his strong arms. Our Love is so alive and uplifting that words to describe it falls short!

Somehow, in this dream, he was showing me again how real his love was. When I saw and felt our joy together, it was so uplifting! I had asked him to come along on our Baja trip and I believe that's one way he chose to make his presence known. Sometimes it takes a few days to process such a dream. I also remember thinking in the dream, 'Well, maybe this bookstore will carry our new book when it's done?' Kevin has encouraged me to write and share our interactions about Love and how it never dies. We are both learning in this process, and we hope that sharing it will make a difference in other people's lives as well.

The only sad part to this dream was the ending. I looked all around for Kevin and finally found him lying under a tree. I knelt next to him and saw tears filling his eyes. "I have to go back, and I don't want to leave you," he said. I cradled the back of his head with my hands and heard, "Ready for coffee?" It was the booming baritone voice of my husband asking. I opened my eyes. "Oh, my God Bryan, I was just with Kevin in my dream time. It was so amazing and real."

It only dawned on me later that the woman in the dream was the same one we had met along the Rio Grande, near Taos, in New Mexico. That was the moment when Kevin made a loud and clear confirmation, by orchestrating an almost impossible encounter, that he was always listening.

The next day, we found the perfect campsite that Santa had described, and it was right on the water's edge. We enjoyed that site for about 10 days.

After my daily meditation and writing sessions, I kept looking across the bay and I was drawn to the other side, and I just wanted to be there for some unknown reason. Hmmm, this was a bit strange. I finally shared these reoccurring thoughts with Bryan and asked him if he would walk around the bay to check it out. At this point, my right knee was bone on bone, so I couldn't walk the full distance. The day before leaving camp, Bryan went to explore the north side of the beach with our dog Kilo and came back with interesting news. He had met a woman who lived there and had a wonderful conversation. After sharing how much we loved Baja, he asked if any home might be for sale. It was such a coincidence as her next-door neighbor had just passed from cancer. The lady offered to give us a tour of the place before we left as she just happened to have a key!

We made our way through the extremely basic bachelor getaway. The house was dark, and all the windows were boarded up. The walls were covered with too many Mexican rugs, but "It has good bones," Bryan said as we drove away. It was solidly built but needed to be a total re-do on the inside! With my background as an interior designer and artist, my mind quickly saw the possibilities. Ten minutes later, we decided to make an offer to the son of the deceased owner, and everything fell into order easily and quickly. This felt like it was meant to be. We looked forward to moving into our new getaway home and putting in the work and love to make it a beauty.

We had found our little slice of heaven in Coyote Bay. There is breathtaking beauty and an abundance of loving energy surrounding our new homestead. Being immersed in nature had always been an important part of my life and I am now grateful to have, once again, time to focus on my writing and art. Will this book I am writing be the one I have envisioned? Time will tell… The squeal of the seagulls and Kilo playing around are distracting me. I had to repeat to myself, "Be open in the now. Just be in the present moment and breathe. Take in the love…feel it, BE IT! Ahhh…"

March 15, 2017

WHAT HAVE YOU LEARNED ABOUT LOVE?

M–"God day Christ, my Angels, and my Kevin in Heaven. I would like Kevin to come through today and see what he has to say about love."

M–"Good morning, Kevin, are you here?"

K–"Yes, Momma, I am!"

M–"Good, I would love to hear what have you have learned about love lately, Kevin."

K–"Sure, that's all there is! I certainly know that, now, from this side. I love the books you are currently reading on the subject. Keep trusting in the Love that you are and the supporting Love Energy that is all around you. While I didn't get this while I was a human, I am glad that you get it, Mom. I know you tried to show me, yet even with all your Angel stories, I was just too stubborn, and I had no knowledge or understanding *that* **HELP WAS REALLY AVAILABLE**. It really was my dark night of the soul. I got lost in feeling that I was a failure in my job and in my relationship and I could not see my way through. My suffering was great, but it caused even more heartache for everyone when I left. *If only* **I HAD TRUSTED IN LOVE!** But I am now here, remembering who I am, Love and Joy."

M–"Love?"

K–"Yep, that's it, Mom. It's so simple and so vast to return to PURE LOVE. There's no judgment, just Love. To feel that, is so freeing."

M–"Well, I always knew that is who you were, from conception to death. Your sweet smile was pure Love and Joy. I am so sorry that you forgot knowing yourself, as Love, while you were here, but it makes me so happy to feel you in this moment and to know that you have returned to your joyous self. You were still learning all about being Love while embodied here. The learning now continues on the other side."

K–"Thanks, Mom. I am glad that you have decided to share our connection with others. Choose Happiness! Choose LOVE! I love the book you're reading, *The Untethered Soul*."

M–"Yes, glad you also like that book. Big hugs of Love to you. Got to go eat some tacos with new friends we met on the beach."

April 16, 2017

REBIRTH

M–"God Day! Christ who resurrected on this Easter Day! My Angels and My Kevin in Heaven!"

"We have now returned from Baja back to our home in Encinitas. After attending a wonderfully inspiring Easter service with Reverend Christian Sorensen at Seaside Center for Spiritual Living, I feel more determined than ever to roll back the stones and continue to be still and listen. I am especially thinking of you, Kevin, and hope you want to speak with me…and us all today. What does rebirth mean to you? I will now breathe and drop into receptivity. Thank You."

"I Love you Kevin, bigger than the expanding Universe!"

K–"I Love you too, Momma."

M–"Good to be in touch on this beautiful day."

K–"Thanks, Mom, for taking the time and courage to reach out."

M–"Of course, my dear. You are always in my heart and mind, even when I don't take time to still myself and listen."

K–"I know, Mom. I am with you so often, even when your thoughts of me have gone by. It's a cool thing that there really is no separation even though I am not in a body."

M–"I asked earlier about your thoughts of rebirth. Can you tell, me how you see that?"

K–"Because we really never die, it is an interesting question. Life and birth, as humans know it, is a Spirit that is reborn into human form. That is amazing right there! It is so beyond our ability to even imagine this gift of life we have been given. The magic of it all coming together to create a life in physical form is awesome."

M–"Yes, I agree. I think of your magical night of conception flying in on a shooting star and nine months later a beautiful baby boy! It is all very amazing to me as well. Continue on…"

K–"It is birth and awakening into form, into a body, with a whole new world of sensations, shapes and colors. It is Love that makes it happen for sure. A bigger Love of Creation that we can't even imagine has created us all. It's beyond just two people coming together and having a moment of passion, but rather the larger urge to keep creating. I would say that's a *God Thing*, a continuum of Love that comes together to create life."

M–"Yes, for sure."

K–"It is Life itself, right here and now, as you and me and each of us experience it, no matter if we are in a body or not. We are a continuum, each of us, in a form, and also when formless. So, to answer your question… Yes, there is always rebirth from Spirit to form as a human and from human to Spirit. It never ends and it is all in the now, intertwined, and inner connected."

M–"Sounds beautiful! So glad you know that. It is good to hear this from you and to know that you understand that you are part of this continuum."

M–"We now need to go join Bryan's family for Easter dinner. We will continue this conversation about life later. I Love you so much. Continue to be in Joy because that's who I know you still are."

K–"Yeah, Mom, Love is the glue!"

M–"So glad we got this my dear!"

Chapter 11

Clever Boy

"She was no longer wrestling with the grief, but could sit down with it as a lasting companion and make it a sharer in her thoughts."
—George Elliot

May 9, 2017

With excitement, we returned to Coyote Bay after a few weeks back home. The owner's son suggested that we live in the house for a couple of weeks before buying it. Our minds were set, but we still accepted this generous opportunity before completing the transaction. Shortly after, we took possession of the house, as it was left, toothbrushes and all, and began a big cleanup.

KEVIN GUIDES US

M–"God Day here in Coyote Bay. It's 73 degrees and the ocean breeze carries refreshing energy. It is now time for me to stop all the 'doingness' of moving into our wonderful house on the beach. I thank my Angels and my Kevin in Heaven for bringing us to this peaceful haven."

"I will finally breathe and let go and ask for any guidance that wishes to come through."

K–"Hey Mom, glad you like the place, Thought you would."

M–"Yes, for sure! It's quite amazing. Glad to know you are here. I thought you might have something to do with this."

K–"Yep, glad Santa Claus directed your search to Coyote Bay."

M–"Me too. I thought it was very interesting… His truck breaking down just 20 minutes after leaving his campsite of four months…and we ended up camped next to him! I loved that he looked just like Santa Claus. I remember when he greeted us that evening. I will not ask *how* you pulled this off Kevin…but thanks for bringing it all together."

K–"You are welcome, Mom. I know you both missed L. A. Bay. You will both find lots of peace, beauty, creativity, and joy being here in this location."

M–"Yes, we are, and thank you so much for all your loving support. We wouldn't have found this place without you; what a gift!"

A year later, after we had found the gift of our Coyote Bay home, there was our Santa, the one who has suggested this area, all dressed up for the children in town. What a great surprise to see him again! I shared with him how he had helped to guide us, along with Kevin. He was overjoyed to hear this.

May 29, 2017

THE GIFTS AND SIGNS

Bryan and I went on a trip to Kauai, Hawaii, to celebrate our fifth wedding anniversary. As we enjoyed this paradise island, the gifts and signs from Kevin continued to appear.

M–"God day on Kauai, Christ, my Angels and my Kevin in Heaven. Please be with me now as I breathe, let go and open for your guidance."

K–"Hey Mom."

M–"Is that you Kev?"

K–"Aloha Mom."

M–"Aloha to you! I hoped you might come along; nice here, right?"

K–"For sure! I do remember coming to the islands once with you, Dad, Arie and Chad. We stayed in Hanalei Bay, in Kauai. It was pretty awesome. Another slice of heaven for sure."

M–"Is it even better than in heaven?"

K–"Kauai comes close, though…but all the elements of beauty, Love and expansion are here. *IT'S ALL GOD and IT'S ALL GOOD!* The more beauty you see, the more you bring in to see. We are gifted with the freedom of perception. Interesting how that works."

LOVE NEVER DIES

M–"Is that the same once we leave our physical reality? Is individual perception as a Spirit our unique expression?"

K–"Yep, that never changes."

M–"It's easy to get that when I am in Kauai or Coyote Bay. Not as easy when I'm not feeling well, and things seem cold and gray. But even in those times, it's a choice I can make to go deeper into feeling the Love and beauty around me. It's also important to feel the cold and gray without judgment or beliefs of that being permanent. Look for the beauty in everything. (As Bryan always says.)"

K–"Yes, Mom, and using the tool of *Infinity Love Process* brings you right to Love. It is amazing how fast it shifts your focus from the struggle and conditioned 'doingness' of life to your ability to hear and see beyond, while remaining connected to your body. Guess we are proof of that."

M–"Yes, for sure. Maybe it would be too confusing if I were always this open. I guess my ability to hear all the time is muted and I am OK with that. But I really think more people could hear if they just took time to slow way down, listen and open their senses. That is why I teach the *Infinity Love Process* and encourage people to sense the loving guidance that is available and waiting. My Angels taught me that many years ago."

K–"Well, even though you can't hear me all the time, I am still with you, and you can feel me."

M–"I love getting little signs and gifts from you. Did you have anything to do with that big new roll of toilet paper on the ground?"

K–"Yep! Thought you would find it funny since you've been going to the bathroom so much."

M–"My intestines seem to be on overdrive. I asked Bryan to go to the store for more toilet paper, but he came back with such small skimpy rolls. I guess you overheard me complaining about that. Too funny! Thanks for that *super-sized roll* just lying there on the ground at the bottom of our stairs. *I knew* that was you! You are *MOST* helpful and remain a true fun-loving Soul."

K–"You make me smile too, Mom. Glad you get my jokes. My love is always with you."

M–"You never cease to amaze me. Keep up the good work and thank you for being such a sweet Spirit. Love you so much."

K–"Love you too."

M–"Keep your signs coming!"

June 10, 2017

COURAGE TO CONNECT

K–"HEY MOM! Yeah, it's me. I didn't want to come in too early, but I see you need to get clear on some things."

M–"I do feel a bit clearer on questions I needed to ask. I am grateful that you and I can connect, yet sad that you are no longer here on earth."

K–"It's OK, Mom, *I know how much you Love me.* I needed to wake up and feel a bigger connection to my Soul. I want to take all the pain you feel away, Mom, but all I can do is reach out and say how sorry I am to have brought you sadness through what I've done. I am sorry that

I saw no other way. I know you can hear and feel that I am more aware of how much I am loved and that I am a part of this Love…the *Oneness* we are all connected to. *I get it now* and want to come back in another lifetime and be *that Love,* that *goodness* in the world."

M–"By God's Grace, I know you will come and spread the Love and Joy that only you can share. This gives me a wonderful feeling. I wish I could end all suffering on this planet, but I can only be responsible for my own. When feeling your hopefulness of a fresh start, I sense that you know life is a great gift, and your Soul continues expanding with Love."

"It is awfully hard as your mother to only have memories of your sweet eyes, your preciousness, and not be able to be with your physical self. I cannot run from these tears and push them away. It is through my courage to feel my loss, then open and be still, that I can experience the Love that is so real between us. Even though I want to run away from my pain, and at times I try to resist my sorrow for days, it only prolongs my suffering."

"Yes, I have to choose to *feel* my emotions and then connect with Love and that takes courage; this I have learned. I *have that courage* and I appreciate that about me. I have a sense of purpose knowing that Love is Eternal and that running away from the emotions keeps me in a place of sadness and separation. I want to help *uplift life of others now* and I believe we are here to do this together."

K–"I Love that, Mom. Let's share this message. Let's remind people of their *goodness and Joy* so they can live it *NOW.* You BE that, Mom! You DO that, Mom. I'll do it with you!"

Chapter 12

In Letting Go Your Heart Expands

"Blessed are those with cracks in their broken heart because that is how the light gets in."
—Shannon L. Alder

June 21, 2017

The relationship I have between each of my three sons is unique and it is changing through the different stages of their lives. As they spread their wings and become independent young men, I see their journey as their own. Distance in miles can make it more challenging to stay connected, to observe them and interact. Thankfully, we now have more opportunities to say I love you and I care for you with a phone call, a text message, or an e-mail. Whatever loving and uplifting words of support come to mind can be shared, such as, *'Keep up the good work.'* Or *'I am sorry you are overwhelmed right now.'* We can express our love however we see fit, so they know that our love is always unconditional. We hope they understand that we are always a 'safe place' for them, a harbor in the storm, when needed.

CONNECTING AS A MOM AND BEYOND

Mothers can often feel when their children are struggling. Consciously or unconsciously, some part of us becomes unsettled and uneasy when something is happening. It's difficult to describe this, but every mom knows exactly what I'm saying.

In *any* relationship, *it takes two.* You can reach out, but it requires the other person to reach back. *The journey of Love* is about *what you can give and not about what you think you need…*

I am also learning to understand the pain I'm feeling when I'm reaching out and it is not being received or the reaching back is less frequent. When my calls, texts or emails aren't returned, the silence of no-replies becomes louder. This brings more concerns and questions to mind, and the heart gets heavier. It may drive me crazy, yet I have learned to have a strong belief in a Powerful and Loving God. I know that the *Presence of Love is Always with My Sons*. I have learned to trust that *Their Process* is the best for their own journey.

Anytime I think of my boys with loving concern, or if I have reached out in thought or action, I mentally say, "I love you. God and your Angels are right where you are." This call, on the Grace of God, brings Peace that passes all understanding.

As a mother, I feel a deep desire for my children to be safe and fulfilled. It brings more questions, though… "Can I let go and Let God do it?", "Can I trust my wisdom?", "Do I genuinely believe that the Grace of God is with my child?" The deepest connection a mother has will always be there since the miracle of life came through her.

When life challenged Kevin, he felt so overwhelmed and stuck with hopelessness, which brought him to withdraw from everyone. He seemed to surface occasionally when he felt good about his new job. *No* one ever thought that the difficulties he was facing would be so overpowering that he would end his own life. NO *ONE,* not even me, his mom!

Someone said to me a long time ago, "Meditation is just taking the time to *let in the Love."* That was such a huge shift for me. *A true light bulb moment!* Letting go of the chatter of the mind and watching it be quieted into a Loving space of receptivity is such a great gift to the self. The ability to watch the chatter and to *ease into being the observer of the mind* is a skill well worth developing. Letting go and expanding awareness provides a feeling of release. One of my favorite books about being the observer and choosing happiness is *The Untethered Soul: The Journey Beyond Yourself,* by Chris Singer.

IN LETTING GO YOUR HEART EXPANDS

> You truly can reach a state in which you never have any more stress, tension, or problems for the rest of your life. You just have to realize that life is giving you a gift, and that gift is the flow of events that takes place between your birth and your death. These events are exciting, challenging, and create tremendous growth. To comfortably handle this flow of life, your heart and mind must be open and expansive enough to encompass reality. The only reason they're not is because you resist. Learn to stop resisting reality, and what used to look like stressful problems will begin to look like the stepping-stones of your spiritual journey (155).

In this process of learning to let go and allowing myself to go into a place of observance and receptivity, I receive answers to all my questions about my concerns or at times the guidance just when I need it. The answers are there, even if it is to simply wait. By the *Grace of God, Love is always present* and in many forms. The more I practice meditation, where I hear and feel the Love, the more aware I become of the continual signs of Love all around me. "Look for the beauty," my husband always says, and it is so true!

Worrying gets you nowhere. My mother is a worrier. She thinks that if you are not worrying, you are not concerned. She feels like it is her job to worry, so she keeps worrying, even at 97 years old. I have noticed that it seems to get worse as she gets older. Happiness is fleeting, at best, and peace is what she hopes to find *after* she dies.

If I am *looking for what is not working,* I can go down a *dark rabbit hole* which is attracting more of what is *wrong* or of what I perceive as not working. I now know that I have a choice. It's my responsibility to live a balanced life.

I Love my body by providing it with good nutrition. I feed my brain and my body with what it needs. I also move to keep it in shape. All these actions are important to feel more vibrant and embodied in the now.

Being in your body is important; otherwise, people remain in their head, making the body follow *conditioned self-orders*. Pick up the pen, walk here, go there, and do that chore. The head acts as a dictator and the body as a slave. Whenever I hear my internal self say, "I have to do…", I know it's a conditioned response. Whenever I feel like I must do something, I realize that I am not making a conscious choice. I want to be aware, awake, and decide how I live my life, instead of reacting unconsciously.

Being in your body is as important as being in Spirit. When I say being in Spirit, I refer to when your consciousness, or your awareness, is of *'Being' (feeling, observing, sensing, choosing) and not conditioned doing*. It is the dance of self-observance about who we truly are, a Spirit carrying a body. We are hosted in this physical gift, the body which we've been given, so our Spirit can choose how to experience life and feel everything through our physical senses intentionally. It is really quite amazing! This is how life is flowing through our physical body. We are here to choose how we perceive our life. There are hundreds of ways to do it, so it's your choice. How do you want to feel? How do you want your experience to be? What are your intentions? What are you saying 'YES' to?

Although we might not realize this, we are in complete control of our perceptions. Our belief system or past experiences might create a lens through which we judge or react to a situation. We might feel like something is done to us, yet we are in control about how we experience it.

That's how you create your life, through your individual and personal perceptions. The utterly amazing thing here is that life is like fingerprints, completely unique for each individual.

I believe God has given us a *freewill zone* here on earth. I have facilitated many sessions with clients and Angels always wanted me to remind them that in this physical zone, *we must always ask* for help. They make it clear that without asking, they will not interfere. It's important to move past our feelings of shame for not knowing something or the pride of our conditioned mind, which believes that you know best. We must ask for guidance or help when needed and know that we deserve the Love and guidance we're seeking. This is where many people get stuck. No matter *what* the situation is, Love and Guidance will be provided once help is requested. Everyone deserves Goodness, Guidance and Grace.

We've all heard amazing stories of how miracles can happen. Someone might even avoid a horrible accident by hearing a voice or feeling an urge to do something. We all know how life can change in an instant. Even extremely hard and difficult changes will always turn out to present a blessing. It may, however, take some time to see or understand what it is. It might be through new learning, new perceptions, or something that you really needed. The important thing to remember is to *keep asking for help*. Everything is here to provide exactly what you need. The other important thing to remember is that you do not always get what you WANT, but you will always get what you NEED. There is often a vast difference between wants and needs. **It is your responsibility to learn about you and what you need to have a life worth living.**

Jesus taught us, "*Knock* and the door will be opened." In other words, "Ask and you shall receive." Ask what you *need* and *know* that it is coming in a way that is even better than what you could have imagined. The great miracle of life is that help is always available. Love is waiting to help and show us the way, but we must ask first. We must also know that we are deserving and be open to receive. Allow the help to show up, be it big or small; it will always happen in amazing ways! Staying open is important as it shows that you simply do not have the answers needed in that moment. Surrender to that awareness and *know* that answers will come in the proper time. There is always a Divine Order.

Much has been written and shared about "the miracles" which I believe are a *normical* occurrence. (That's a word from my dear friend Phyllis Brown that you won't find in the dictionary!)

> **Normical:** An answer, a direction, or a healing that happens to help someone move away from a problem.

Why will these normical 'miracles' happen? Because this Love, which *is you*, and connected *with you*, is ready to help and return you to the awareness of the wholeness that you are.

I believe there is nothing too big or too small when asking for help from the other side. I remind myself that my Highest Spirit is present within and connected to all of creation. The best answers will always come to my rescue in Divine timing. The frustrated or stressed-out version of me needs to let go when it doesn't have a clue. We are not weaker by asking for direction and help. We are stronger together because we are *One with Divine Intelligence and Wisdom*. The more we practice this dance, the more magical it gets. It's like watching your own life unfold in wonderful ways.

WHY WOULD WE NOT ASK?

June 23, 2017

MY TIMING

M– "OK, my Kevin in Heaven, time to connect? I am ready. How about you?"

K– "Yeah, Mom, just been waiting for you."

M– "Ha-Ha! Yes, things can get in the way. I've set my boundaries up and now choose to have conversations only when I am ready. I am turning off the phone and closing the door energetically on the busy energy around me. I am grateful that Bryan is respectful of my time as well."

"I love you so very much and I always love connecting, but I have begun to realize that I've been putting our time off. I am not always ready to feel my deep emotions when they emerge. My sadness that you are so close and yet so far can seem unbearable at times. Do you understand this? I am also uplifted and amazed by your answers and by your perspective on things! It is a gift beyond measure; a gift we have been given by God."

K–"Yes, Mom, I know. I want to be here only if you want me. I know it has taken a lot of courage and strength for you to get to this place. I love you so much, Mom, and I see and feel when you are ready, and I respect that."

M–"Thank You, Honey. I think you also feel when I am tired and my focus fades."

K–"Yep, I get it."

M–"Right now I am a bit anxious about the call I need to make to the renters of our Idyllwild house. I feel better, though, just connecting and being clear about how powerful and precious our sharing is. I also appreciate that you understand my timing."

"My intention is to stay open and connected so we can have more conversations about Love and what you are learning. Please continue to be there for Arie in any way you can. *Love you as big as the expanding Universe.*"

K–"Love you too, Mom, 'till next time."

I closed my journal and immediately made the call to our renters. Bryan and I were feeling it was time to sell that property. It was a hard decision for me because this home was so special. It was perched on a wonderful private outlook on the mountain range. It was my place of healing and I shared it with so many others. Now that we lived in Encinitas, we couldn't afford both homes. Our renters had been most ideal in every way. To my amazement, the renter said that he had just found a smaller home that he wanted to buy. He was going to call me but was a bit anxious because he did not want to disappoint us. The irony of it all made me happy and relieved! I love how that was clearly in *Divine Order,* and a result of staying open to being Loved.

Chapter 13

The Illusion of Separation

*"Everyone wants to live on top of the mountain,
but all the happiness and growth occurs while
you're climbing it."*
—Andy Rooney

From the grandeur of the High Sierras, I was inspired by the Love we shared as a family. It was a magnificent place and the perfect time to have a chat with Kevin about a concept he shared called the God Glue of Love.

July 27, 2017

OPEN TO THE GOODNESS

M–"God day! Here we are at Lake Thomas Edison, up in the High Sierras, camping with all our kids. I have felt the Love. I open now for you, Kevin, to come in… I will breathe and let go…"

"Hey Kevin, hope you have been enjoying all the joy down here."

K–"Hey Mom! Very cool to see and feel the Love. I am with you all. So much fun the annual Bagley Family Talent Show and seeing everyone so involved. Glad Chad and Jamie made it too. Sorry Arie couldn't make it as well."

M–"You know I think of you often, hoping you are a part of it somehow."

K–"Well, I am. Remember, there is no separation. We are all connected. The God Glue is working. Always will…and never ends."

M–"It's only the *illusion of separation* that seems to disconnect us. I know it is on me; I have to be still and truly let go to be able to listen. Thank goodness I know how to get grounded and open up to receive. I always find it amazing that *you* are *here when I do the work to get out of the way.*"

K–"It's the *God Glue* and *Love* that makes the connection possible."

M–"So glad you get it Kev, and I love the *God Glue* concept. You said earlier that the connection is possible because I forgave you for ending your physical life and that opens the channels to speak and share our Love."

K–"What you, as a human, and I, as a spirit, have right now is forever. That Love and connection we had with each other on Earth and have beyond never ends. *Our Love never ends*…that's the magic of it all. If only I could have seen that while I was there! But I am learning that it is never too late to evolve. Everything becomes a whole lot easier when we know that we are Love. It is *the conditioned mind's beliefs* that get in the way of being open to that truth. Things always work out. *Keep learning* and realize that you are in a place of *Love and Support.* Just open your heart to GOD and *GOODNESS. Life is Good, if you let it be*…and even if that is not your present experience…*the GOOD still IS.*"

M–"I get it, Kev. Open to the goodness and the goodness flows. Thank you, Kevin, for your insights from the other side. I am getting hot sitting in the sun since it moved above the treetops. It is a delight to hear you and be with you. Until we talk again, know that you are loved and missed here. Enjoy your Heavenly journey until we come together again."

K–"Right, Mom. Love you too."

August 8, 2017

MOVING ON

M–"God day here on the mountaintop of Idyllwild. I will now breathe, let go and open to my Angels and my Kevin in Heaven. What do you have to share with me about this move and selling my home of 25 years?"

K–"Hey Mom."

M–"Hey right back to you. You have been hanging out and seeing what's happening?"

K–"Yep, such an awesome place to have lived. Glad you hung on to it for so many years, Mom. It was home, the only real home I felt good in. I think that's because you were always making it *home*. Lots of great cooking we did too, Mom. That was so much fun."

M–"Some of my favorite memories are with you here when you moved back as a Junior in High School, and we cooked meals together."

K–"Hard to leave this beautiful mountain view, right?"

M–"It sure is. The energy and beauty will always be inside me. It will be part of me, and I will have deep gratitude for having been here."

K–"It will always be a part of me too, Mom. I love you and don't want you to be sad about letting it go. From here, it feels right. I think it's a good time to sell. You can feel good about it coming together. Bryan is giving it some love and it's looking great."

M–"Yes, that's it. Giving it some love and detailing it out."

K–"Just remember, everything is temporary and you'll be heading to Coyote Bay, after next week's knee replacement surgery, right after you're done with physical therapy. Lots to look forward to, Mom. It's not over for you yet."

M–"Ha-Ha! No, it's not over yet. There is a lot more living to do."

K–"Live it fully and *look for the beauty,* as Bryan says. So glad you are with him. Tell Bryan I am with you both and I'm so happy you are together. He is a good man and I see how much you love him, and how he loves you. It's great to see Chad and Jamie together too. They are both good for each other. I was watching them on their trip to Kauai. Great place for lovers, right Mom?"

M–"Yes, it wasn't too long ago when Bryan and I were there for our 5th Wedding anniversary. Yes, that place is unique to my heart, just like this mountain top here, but you are more special than all of this. Thank you, Kevin, for our ongoing connection. I'm already looking forward to the next time."

K–"Me too, Mom, take care and keep your chin up. I'm with you always."

M–"I am with you too…the place in my heart that can never be taken away."

K–"That's it, Mom, never!"

M–"Love you as big as the expanding Universe!"

K–"Love you too. *IT'S ALWAYS IN LETTING GO THAT YOUR HEART EXPANDS!*"

August 20, 2017

AN OPENING, NOT AN ENDING!

M–"God day, Angels, Guides, and my Kevin in Heaven. It is my last day here in this beautiful home on the mountaintop of Idyllwild. Please bring me a message and soothe my Soul about leaving this wonderful place as it goes on the market."

"You have lived upon the mountaintop and grown in your awareness while working with the Earth Energy and Spiritual Energy to become who you are today. You are wiser and more compassionate in your understanding and willingness to be a conduit to help others to clear and open to the Love that they are. This has happened because of your obvious choice to go beyond your seeming limitations and fears."

"It is time now to spread your wings and fly. Take all that you are and all that you have learned to a new expression of Spirit. Trust the unfoldment of your healing, in your meditations, in your writing and sharing with others."

"This mountain has been your place of learning and healing. Trust in the unseen to manifest. We have always been here for you, and we will continue to help you in your moving forward. You leave nothing behind but the past. You move forward with the *fullness of trust* and *knowing* that you are connected to the Oneness, Love, Wisdom, and you have the ability to share this in many ways. You are not done, but opening and trusting once again that selling your home, here in Idyllwild, will always bring a fuller expression of you as you let go… The energy here will always be with you and a part of who you are. No one or nothing can take that away."

LOVE NEVER DIES

"Fear not my Dear One...but *trust this is an opening not an ending!* Give it to God! Thy will be done on Earth as it is in Heaven... Go with peace and joy..."

"Thank You, Archangel Michael!"

> *"There are far, far better things ahead than anything we leave behind."*
> —C. S. Lewis

Chapter 14

Being in the Flow

"We must embrace pain and burn it as fuel for our journey."
—Kenji Miyazawa

Working through the pain and difficulties, beyond my present limitation, I was being reminded of my inner strength by my Kevin in Heaven. What a powerful gift to be lifted to such a level. It resonated through me beyond the words that he spoke. I felt a deep letting go and knowing, once again, that the healing was happening at many levels.

October 3, 2017

DON'T LET THE PAIN STOP YOU

M–"God Day, Christ, my Angels, Guides, and my Kevin in Heaven. I will breathe, let go and open to my connection to Spirit. Thank You…"

K–"It's going to be OK Mom. I am here and have been with you all the way. So sorry it's been so hard being in your body, but you are going to get better and better. It is time to fully take care of you, just as *putting on the oxygen mask first,* so you can then be there for others. I Love you Mom, and from here I can see that you are surrounded in Love. And let's be real, Bryan's Love is strong, even when he seems distant. He cares and he is there for you. That's a gift, and you deserve it. I know you feel a bit sad when working through the physical pain, but you are strong, Mom. You know this will pass, even though it seems slow, and then your creativity will come back. Be gentle with yourself. Imagine it is me going through it and what would you want me to know and do?"

M–"Right, honey. I can see this is only temporary and I know this surgery will help me walk better. *No one* tells you how painful it's going to be ahead of time, yet I know that it's only temporary. It is the beginning of October here, and I have a month to prepare. I will focus on showing up for myself with diet, exercise, meditation and being as strong as *you* see me. Thank you for that."

K–"You are welcome, Mom. You are so strong. I will never forget how strong you were to stand up in front of almost 300 people at my Memorial and be so open and real...that is *STRONG!* You pulled it off, even when your heart felt so broken from what I did. You are strong because you come from your heart and won't let the pain stop you from taking the next step. You moved through the pain without running away from it; that's huge. You know there is more for you to express and do, but remember it needs to come from your heart. That is the Love you know yourself to be. Trust that you are connected to so much more Love, wisdom, and support that guides your way. I see it takes courage to go beyond what seems like limitations...physically or emotionally and *reach beyond...that is strength.*"

M–"I will let that in Kevin, in the midst of my doubts and fears."

K–"Yes, Mom, it is OK right now because *you are Love* and you allow your human self *not to be limited.* Limitation is the illusion. No matter how real we think it is or how painful it is...going beyond the pain and believing that you can move into something even better is strength. When limiting thoughts stop, *something better* will grow larger and larger and replace the smallness you feel right now. Suffering happens when you believe and feel those limitations as if that's all there is. Remember, even though your pain is real, it will pass with time. Be open to having everything work out, even when you are in the thick of it! It is humanities' work to move through challenges and learn about the goodness that wants to express through each person."

M–"Don't limit my good, right? Keep expanding beyond."

K–"Yes, Mom, go beyond your limited mind that thinks it can figure it all out."

M–"That's the trap, the mind trying to figure everything out."

K–"Yep, you limit yourself and don't even realize you are creating your limitations. Yet there are so many more possibilities than what your mind knows to work things out."

M–"So, it's like relaxing all thoughts around any troubling situation, letting the mind rest, and accepting that you don't have the answers. Watch all thoughts that arise and catch them before they give back a conditioned answer. Let all conditioning be suspended while goodness replaces old brain patterns. Keep focusing on what you need while letting go completely of all thoughts around what is *NOT* working. New brain waves take hold and that's when miracles happen — the creation of a new and beautiful outcome. It's the Law of Attraction…"

K–"That's it! Let the good happen, let the healing continue and stay open so the goodness can flow."

M–"Thank you my dear, I am with you always."

K–"I'm with you too, Momma."

This chat with Kevin makes think of a powerful talk Bryan and I heard at Seaside Center for Spiritual Living. Reverend Christian Sørensen's message that day was "The Way It Works." It had such a strong impact that I have listened to the replay immediately upon returning home to take a few notes.

He reminded us of the words from Ernest Holmes in 1938:
> *"Life must contain two fundamental characteristics. We shall see there is an Infinite Spirit operating through an Infinite and Immutable Law. In this Cosmos and not chaos, finds an eternal existence and Reality. Love points the way and Law makes the way possible." (Science of Mind Textbook, 43.)*

In essence, you apply this into your life by planting the seed of your thoughts and desires and allowing the fertile soil to manifest what you have planted. It is the scientific Law of cause and effect. What Christ said eons ago, "It is done to you as you believe," still holds this truth.

You must become the observer and notice the thoughts and feelings limiting you. Those can lead to conscious or unconscious beliefs which can limit the expression of your true essence. This awareness is the first door you step through to free yourself and get to the truth of who you are. That's why I keep repeating, "Watch your stinking thinking and embrace your right to be happy."

Rev. Christian also brought our attention to these words:
> *"Therefore, our belief sets the limit to our demonstration of a Principle which, of Itself, is without limit. It is ready to fill everything, because it is Infinite. So, it is not a question of Its willingness, nor of Its ability. It is entirely a question of our own receptivity." (Science of Mind Textbook, 37.)*

Infinite Wisdom and Intelligence is always here; to me that Is God. One of the favorite mantras I say to myself is "God is here, all is well." It is through our intuition and listening that we receive our guidance and answers.

> *"The Thing, then, works for us by working through us and is us, always. It cannot work for us in any other way."*
> —Ernest Holmes

January 18, 2018

RETURN TO THE FLOW

K–"Did I hear you, Mom?"

M–"Yes, I am here. It's been a while. It is me that must slow down and tune in."

K–"Yep, you are a busy bee getting ready to go back to Coyote Bay. This is good. I see you happy, creating and doing healing work with others. It is your place of peace and love. Happy to have brought Santa Claus to you so you could find it. See, because you were listening to what felt good, like not being in the truck any longer, then Bryan could remember the hotel in Mulegé. Isn't it fun how things just come together? Focus on what feels good."

M–"Yes, it is fun to be open and not set about how it *should be*… I'm so grateful Bryan is also in the flow."

K–"Yes, I heard you talking last night about being in your bliss. I think you do a great job of that. Meditating a bit more would be good…"

M–"I am with you there. Man, I can get caught up in the 'doingness' of life. It's so easy, especially back here in the energy of Encinitas. I find city energy to be buzzing and I'm not fond of this… I can get worn out quickly."

K–"There is no judgment around that 'doingness.' Remember, the mind makes that up. It's more about what works better in the moment and choosing to move in the direction you intend. I see people do get so hung up in 'doingness,' and spiraling down, which means further from ease, instead of being in the flow, and spiraling up."

M–"Oh boy, I get that, Kevin! So glad you see it. Don't you wish we could come into this life already knowing and doing that?"

K–"Yet, humanity is here to learn they *can live in the flow,* that's called life. Some just struggle more than others and you, Mom, are here to remind them of this flow… *The Divine Flow!"* Once learned and fixed into the structure of human bodies, in the DNA, then future humans will have this pattern available. It will have been adopted for themselves and life will be far easier.

M–"Yes, thank you. Sometimes I get so busy in life that I forget and fall into my conditioned reactions of how to live. I start thinking that I *need* to do this; I *need* to do that; or when I'm finished here, I'll start doing that. Functioning from what I believe I must do, rather than what I want to do, limits me. Making life about what I think must be done, rather than about what I want to do, keeps me from evolving. I am truly most happy when I am consciously connecting to God, my Angels and to you now in the Spirit World. I still realize that I have places in me functioning from my rules, beliefs, and conditioning. I continue to work on my awareness to make more conscious choices. I want my creative force to be flowing in my life and moving me away from conditioned, or limited thinking. When I fully grasp this wisdom, I will continually be connected to my Spirit, which is united to All that is. I am still a work in progress."

K–"Sometimes, getting busy in life feels great. When you are in the flow of life, *surrendered* in the moments of doing, that is a lovely sensation. But when you're busy in your mind, overthinking and forcing decisions about what to do or how to do it, that's when the flow stops. When you find yourself doing anything you DON'T want to do, that can also slow your flow. Find ways to consciously choose to do everything, instead of reacting. Remember you choose your perceptions and when you make yourself a victim to life you reject God, for being a victim was never intended for you. Love never creates a victim."

M–"Life does have exceedingly difficult times, so how does one not become victimized by that?"

K–"Give yourself time to be with the situation. You decide what outcome you would want. Then, you choose what actions you want to take to achieve your outcome. If you have no idea how to proceed, that's when you ask for help and acknowledge that you do not have your answers. When you simply surrender, and ask for help, your wisdom or Higher Self knows there is always a perfect answer waiting for you. Staying open, quiet and waiting, will bring that help. You know what happens when you ask yourself a question and allow space to receive? That space of waiting is being open for your answers. It's literally a physical feeling and that's how you will determine if you are open to receive help. It's a quiet and peaceful space, yet very enjoyable once understood. It's really important to practice this in your daily life and use it with all your small choices. When big events happen in your life, which can throw you off your pivot, you will then have a method of behavior that will fully support you. This is how to stay connected, to not only God, but also to your higher wisdom."

M–"Thanks Kev for sharing your wisdom and thoughts. What a gift you are."

K–"Now that you have a new granddaughter, Brinkley, you can fully share your love, wisdom and truth with her."

LOVE NEVER DIES

M–"Great, so glad you see that. It is a wonderful gift to have her in this family. We are all blessed."

K–"Yes, she is a special Soul, as you will see…"

M–"Until our next time. Love you more than the expanding Universe!"

K–"Love you too, Momma. Thanks for taking the time."

M–"My pleasure."

K–"My Joy."

May 2, 2018

BEING CONSCIOUS

M–"God day! It is my birthday, and I am spending it here, in Coyote Bay. I call in all the Love to be with me now. Do you have any message for me in my 68th year? Thank You."

K–"Hi ya, Momma! Happy Birthday!"

M–"Thanks Kev. I'm happy to hear from you."

K–"Yes, I am here. Haven't *gone away*. I have been here, there, and everywhere."

M–"So cool you can be a fully multidimensional being, here now and *free* to explore. Is that a good way to put it? Explore?"

K–"Yes. I like to explore but on a *GRAND* scale. There is no end, just an expanding continuum…

M–"Is there a purpose to it all?"

K–"Expansion, beyond feeling stuck with the old, and moving beyond to experience the Collective and realizing our individual place in that Collective."

M–"Our individual purpose?"

K–"No, it's our realization of being Love. Believing you have a Purpose is an earthly human concept...an old one that is limiting. This belief that one must have a purpose limits expansion, investigation, and experimentation in self-awareness. A desire to experience would be a better way to perceive what humans call purpose. The concept of purpose gave our ancestors a reason to begin self-exploration. It was one of many beliefs they followed for their life to make sense. Everything was, and still is, just a stepping stone to awareness. It was useful then, and now it's limiting. It's not about purpose, rather it is always about *being conscious*. Being in a physical body on earth is simply another experience to become more aware of who you are, a loving creation, connected to all that *IS*.

M–"Can connection be felt from this place here and now?"

K–"Yes, in a body or also out, as I am. You are not separate or incomplete, despite the challenges of life on Earth, which is a learning and a joyous experience. Every dimension available to creation is for an experience; it's simply a new dimension for a new perspective, which in turn, gives an opportunity for expansion. So, a Soul, that carries a body, or one in Spirit, no matter where they exist in the moment, is experiencing a new reality. It's simply an opportunity to create their perspective. They can then choose what holds value for them, but they can also just simply enjoy the experience. This is also about learning to simply relish the experience. When one realizes their

Beingness, they will return to a higher perspective and see themselves more fully. All is always well and that will become apparent with bringing Heaven on Earth. It is about returning to the mountain top from a higher perspective of who we really are. Not from a want or need, but an actual feeling at the deepest level that *all is well*. That is the Bliss, **All Is Well**. It is awakening to self.

M–"I am feeling into the words and between the thoughts that you share with me. You do a really good job, by the way."

K–"Thanks Mom. My present is to remind you to *BE THE BLISS,* and to know that *All is Well*. Practice the stillness and let it all go. Just be it."

M–"That's a great gift, Kev. I hear you and feel your Bliss. I have called it 'Practice the Presence and then the Presents show up!' You are my present and I thank you, my Dear. Enjoy the Bliss and I will too."

K–"Love ya, Mom!"

M–"Love you too!"

"Practice the Presence and then the Presents show up!"
—Janice Hope

May 25, 2018

IS IT OVER?

M–"God day, and so it is. I now draw near me my Angels and my Kevin in Heaven. I want to continue hearing about Love, life, and the hereafter."

"It has been almost a month since I have heard from Kevin. I wonder if it is over. Did he need to move on *or* is it me not tuned in enough? Is my communication with Kevin over?"

Then the message came....

"He is quiet for now because he wants you to write the book, '*Love Never Dies.*' It is his way of saying, 'The balls in your court, Mom!'"

M–"HMMM…"

Chapter 15

Opening to Feelings

"Let go. Why do you cling to pain? There is nothing you can do about the wrongs of yesterday. It is yours to judge? Why hold on to the very thing which keeps you from hope and love?"
—Leo Buscaglia

It was our 7th annual family camping trip at the beautiful June Lake in the High Sierras. I found myself sitting under a powerful and gigantic cedar tree, enjoying some alone time.

June 15, 2018

SLOWING DOWN

M–"God day! I breathe and open to *all* your Love."

"Be still and know. The cooing of the dove…the squawking of the blue jays…the chirping of the black birds…the chatter of the squirrels…the breeze is soft… *I Am*."

And then I heard Kevin's voice once again…

K–"I am with you, Momma. Not in a body to feel the breeze, yet I am in the flutter of the leaves. You can feel me in the drop of the rain upon your neck or in the gentle breeze that blows across your face, I am in it all. You have found me, once again, yet I am always here. You look to see me, but I cannot be seen. Breathing into this moment *I AM, WE ARE.*"

M–"I Love you, Kevin."

K–"I Love you too, Momma."

June 18, 2018

IT'S ALWAYS UP TO ME

Sometimes, I find myself swallowed up by a busy life. It is something I still need to work on. I notice that when I stop believing the stories about what I 'have to' do, and start looking at what I want to create, I then stay in the flow of life. It helps to literally ask myself before each action, "what do I want to create?" That question takes the patterned belief of *"I have to"* out of the equation and keeps me more aware. This is a new pattern that takes time to set. If I start my day with this statement, "I'm going to do exactly what I want today," it begins a flow and it's important to learn to stay in that stream. It may be a life's work for me to fully embrace staying in the flow. I know it's completely *up to me* to choose.

As I sit by this beautiful mountain lake, I am full of gratitude. I have taken time out from the family activities, so the hike will go on without me. I needed my time alone to go within.

OPENING TO FEELINGS

I have found my way back to peace and oneness, as I let go and become present in the moment. This is a gift I will always be eternally grateful for. I am thankful for my spiritual deepening and opening; for not feeling separate but deeply connected. There are no words powerful enough to describe such an expanding feeling of Love. I return to a place that *passes all understanding, where* Love can be felt deeply. *It's always up to me.*

It was over 40 years ago when I had the '*Aha* moment' and I felt a huge shift inside about meditation. I was told it was a time to just slow down and LET THE LOVE IN. It wasn't about having no thoughts. That seemed to be so simple. It was time to let the Love in. I wish I could remember who said it, but I got it. The wisdom asked for in meditation is given and peace is found. It is available and offered to all of us, permanently waiting and yet always surprising us by its many forms.

Wisdom comes through My Higher Self, Christ, my Angels, Guides and through so many other signs given by Great Spirit. Hearing what makes no sound and seeing those who have passed onto the other side are gifts that I refer to as Grace. This life is a journey for discovering who we are and what is ours. We have an opportunity to experiment and discover what works for us. Self-Discovery is Magical.

February 15, 2019

I CAN'T FIX IT!

My husband was recently diagnosed with a congenital heart abnormality. When the head Cardiologist of Scripps Hospital said, "We can't fix this, it's too risky," my heart sank! I walked out of his office and went into momentary shock! "Bryan, there's got to be a way!", I said, crying as we held each other.

This shock turned out to be a gift for me because it ripped me down to a core issue, remembering the pain of not being able to do anything about someone else's suffering. This ran deep in me. I felt it as a child with a manic-depressive father and a deeply unhappy mother, but it even went back further than that. Feeling helpless to change another's suffering has been a pattern from lifetimes before. As a child, I couldn't be happy enough, pretty enough, sweet enough or simply be or do enough, to make a real difference.

In my adult life, when I was faced with feelings of helplessness, I would automatically run my 'doingness' pattern to find what I could fix. This was running from a desire to shift or change things in a deeper way. By returning to the *deepest Love that we are, which can transform and heal* in the most profound ways, I continue to find my healing. This is what I have been trying to learn for lifetimes…practicing the Presence of Love and returning to this place of Peace. From there, *all* is given, and has always been given… It has been my journey to *return to the Love that we are, and that we are connected with, in all ways!*

Thank You to All That Is!

March 26, 2019

WHERE'S YOUR HEART?

I wrote the opening in my meditation journal, as I always do. I did my Infinity Love Process Breath, dropped into the stillness, and there's Kevin's voice, once again…

M–"Hey Kevin, what do you think about me finding out who your heart recipient is? A part of me would like to reach out."

K–"Hey Mom. My true heart is with you. You will not find me there, in someone else's body, but here, always with you, always loving you, and always ready to help you any way I can. *YOU have my heart!*"

M–"Oh, that makes me tear right up, Kevin! You are so sweet. Tears are mixed with Love, yet the loss is still here. Your words and Love are always inspirational at the deepest level. I am always grateful for this connection."

K–"Me too, Momma. I am so sorry for the pain, but I am grateful for your *openness to feel our Love* and not shut it down because of the pain. Be happy, Mom. It's OK to cry, just return to the Love and let that inspire you. I am so proud of you and the Love you bring to the world. We are both growing, and I thank you so much for loving me beyond the pain… You're awesome, Mom. *You are meant to share that Love Never Dies!"*

M–"Yes, Kev. Love is a powerful thing, and I believe it is a gift we have all been given. We just need to tune into this frequency and allow that expansion within. Keep showing me the way. Help me be courageous, and help me to express it…"

K–"OK, Mom, you got it! Choose happiness."

M–"Thanks my Dear, I am."

Chapter 16

Expanded Frequencies

"When you move beyond consciousness, you caress the beloved. When you move into the unknown, beyond everything, the beloved caresses you."
—Rumi

Life is an opportunity for expansion, and I continue to learn more about the evolution of the Soul with the help of Kevin. He shared that he missed the humility to seek wisdom and professional guidance while he was here. Sadly, he also didn't have the emotional maturity to dive within and seek his own answers.

April 19, 2019

THE NATURE OF OUR SOUL

M–"God day! I am here in Coyote Bay, fully open to the Christ Light of Love, my Angels, Guides, and my Kevin in Heaven."
"Sorry, I've been so busy."

K–"No worries, Mom, I get it. I am always here when you are ready."

M–"Thanks, Kev. Love you so much. So, what's happening on the *other side?*"

K–"Just being, with all the loving Souls here. We are all expanding together, all learning and *feeling our Oneness,* or *expansiveness* might be the best word to describe it, I guess."

M–"So, *if* you come back into a body, do you bring this expanded sense of being with you?"

K–"I sure hope so."

M–"Me too. So, as a soul, we keep evolving in each incarnation here and there?"

K–"Yes, each at our own level. The Love that is us, and which made us, expands like a flower seed planted on earth and maturing into a blossom."

M–"Beautiful thought."

K–"That's *putting it simply, of course,* because a seed planted will only be that seed's expression. A rose can never be a carnation. As a Soul, we are planted with Love and the *nature or seed of our Soul* chooses its path, but only from the choices of its nature. Each choice is ours to make and we continue expanding or becoming more of what we are."

M–"OK, let's get back to the statement about 'The nature of our Soul.'"

K–"We evolve according to the level of our perceptions. Each life corresponds with the level of consciousness carried, and that is then the nature of that soul. The perspectives you carry as a Soul moves you into life circumstances, environments and situations which creates a perfect *setup* for what you are needing. You are the source for setting up your life and, of course, all guidance requested will be given. You are always the director of your life."

M–"Does that include your parents, environment, location and opportunities, available or not?"

K–"Yep, to all of it! You have full command to all your set-ups, so you can follow the Love and support that is always given to help you move forward in your expanding consciousness. You even have an expansion of consciousness when choosing a more difficult life or path than before."

M–"So, when some parents are not able to express Love, perhaps, that's because they were not fully evolved and were struggling to wake up themselves?"

K–"Yep, everyone is playing out a role, expressing their nature. Then people come together, through some type of relationship, to have an opportunity to wake up and learn about Love and about themselves. We all can make choices towards that, or not. In other words, *it has all been given;* it's just that each of us chooses how it's used. Remember what your spiritual teacher Hazel Denning said? *'It's not important what happens to you, it is more important how you react to it.'*"

M–"Of course."

K–"That is the gift we've been given…free will and the soil in which to grow. Our only limitation is our degree of consciousness or awareness, which is what constitutes our nature. Yet, as a Soul, our ability to express is so vast, it never feels limiting. We are able to choose expansion at all times and on every plane of existence, for it is all part of a Soul's Whole Life. We are always supported by Love because we Are Love. Yet, as a Soul carrying a body, one does feel limitations at times. These are opportunities to expand and reach for help and answers. Which, I now see, are always available."

M–"Thank you, Kevin. Wish we all knew that consciously. It would make life a whole lot easier. I have an appointment with a client in ten minutes. Got to go for now and take this all in. Love you!"

K–"Love you too, Momma."

June 24, 2019

MIND MELTING

M–"OK, Kevin, I *now open to connecting with you fully*. I had a bad fall, and I am in pain, so bear with me. Am I hearing you here?"

K–"Yes, I am here, Mom. Sorry you are hurting so much. You'll get through this. It is hard for you to set time aside. It is your choice, but I think it would be less uncomfortable for you to make the time to connect. Our connection brings you the feelings of Love and taps you into something that is beyond human suffering. It brings you to the core of Love itself, which moves through us. When taking time to enter into that Love, through meditation, or even with any quiet moment, we enter into the awareness *that our Love Never Dies*. We then remember that is where healing, insights and true 'knowing' comes from. In Surrendering we are found. In Knowing, we let go. In Letting Go, there are no boundaries to Love…no restraints…nothing holding us back."

M–"Not even pain can block me from this peace and connection. I haven't felt my pain at all since you started talking."

K–"Well, *it started with you* taking time to breathe into your Infinity Love Process and being still and calm enough to listen."

M–"It feels like the *Grace of Love*. I would call it connecting to *All that IS,* because it feels larger and more expansive than just the loving gift of connecting to each other. It is as if we opened a door and entered into an *expanded frequency* of Peace and Love, from there everything else falls away."

K–"Yes! To be connected in Love is *Mind Melting*. I am waking up to this with you too, Mom. The more we can move past the pain, the more I awaken to the freedom and Joy available. I wish I would have known that while I was *IN a* body."

M–"Me too!"

K–"I did not know how or when to surrender and ask for help. Instead, I fell into limited thinking where there was no escape from suffering… To end my life, as I knew it, seemed the only option at that point. I did not have enough knowledge or life experience to get through difficult situations."

"I am so sorry I did not seek help beyond my own thinking. I did not seek the wisdom of others. I could not even get past my pride about having deep troubles. I thought I would not LOOK GOOD if I didn't have my own answers, so I never asked for help."

"**I left a life not only with my pain but also with the awareness of the pain I caused to others.** *I would now say that suicide is never the way out!* I guess that is one of the reasons why I want you to share this message with others. Just because I did not see *how* I could move from being so unhappy with myself, it doesn't mean there wasn't a life of happiness waiting around the corner."

"If I had only allowed myself *the humility*… I could have spared my life and the suffering of so many I love."

"That was the trap. I thought it was all up to me to figure it out; how to find another job and how to be in a healthier relationship. It was also the fear of not being good enough. I was thinking with pride under the false belief that I needed to *have it all together.*"

"*NOW,* I see there were many possibilities. If only I had reached out to you, to Dad, to my brothers, a counselor or even a suicide prevention hotline… But that would have meant *being **real** with myself and not running away…*"

"I tried to push past the pain and stress of thinking I had to figure it all out. So, I started drinking and smoking a lot, yes pot too. I was just trying to feel some relief and it only brought me down more."

"So, know Mom, the physical pain that is slowing you down only needs time to heal. I am sorry you are crying but you have *so much to give, so much joy to share*. You can do this! Be who you were meant to be, Love and Joy, and share it with others. Remember the little plaque on your bedroom wall? *'Life is a gift and what you do with it is a gift to all creation.'*"

M–"Yes, sharing my love with you is such a gift. Thank you, Kev. I will continue to move forward in bringing this message out into the world. This is my gift to give, and you will always be a gift to me. Thank You!"

K–*"No, thank you, Mom for being you* and for being on the path of Love. Take time to reach out beyond the pain. *Love you as big as the expanding Universe!"*

M–"Same to you, my dear and thank you for our connection… *Love Never Dies!"*

July 16, 2019

EXPANSION

M–"God day Christ, my Angels, Guides, and my Kevin in Heaven. I let go and I am now open to speaking with Kevin… What would you like to talk about?"

K–"Hey ya, Mom, so glad you are back in the mountains with the peace and without all the busy city energy."

M–"I love being here with Bryan and our extended family. The three children and seven grandkids are here for our annual family camping trip again."

K–"Yes, it is a great family for sure. I would have enjoyed them, but it makes me happy for you that you have them, and they have you."

M–"Aww, thank you, my dear. So, what would you like to share with me? What new awareness are you experiencing on the other side?"

K–"I would say *EXPANSION*..."

M–"OK."

K–"On Earth, I was *very unaware* of the ability to go beyond my mind, except when smoking pot by myself. I could go into a happier place, feel a sense of expansion, and I was more connected to everything. Yet, that was only temporary relief."

"I didn't get that I could go within and ask for any guidance or wisdom... I didn't realize the amazing possibilities, or the Love I could connect with. I missed out while I was in a body and got too caught up. My responses and beliefs about happiness and life were conditioned by the world around me. I only knew what I knew and never did seek wisdom outside or inside of myself."

M–"I hear that, Kevin. I wonder if our being able to connect is some part of knowing that."

K–"For sure, Mom. I see you intentionally taking time out to be still and in this is how you experience inner peace. You open your awareness and bring that into your physical body, as all the Love that is around, and within. You have the wisdom to let go of your conditions, just be open to be still and listen."

M–"Yes, Kevin. I am so grateful and also delighted with surprise that Love, wisdom, and guidance show up in so many ways. It is in my personal relationship with God/Love, with Christ, my Angels… It also shows through my ability to tune into loved ones on the *other side or* when helping a client. It is always amazing to receive and share this gift."

"To expand beyond my pain of missing you, and actually be involved in interesting and enlightening conversations with you, takes my ability to expand to a whole new level."

K–"The *inner wisdom* has always been available, and everyone can tap into it. Each of us can chose a path to learn and expand."

M–"Life is an automatic journey to self. It offers many avenues to find Love, happiness, and deep fulfillment. That is a gift! Some use it to seek expansion and others not so much. Nevertheless, all are given exactly what is needed to discover what they choose to open to. Each person gets to choose what they want from life. It is their responsibility to awaken and express themselves as the pure Love they are."

K–"There are two opposing ways of living as human, the outer life, survival through conditioning, or *being in the flow of awareness*. It should become an automatic reflex to recognize in which state you are. Is it flowing with ease or are you following a conditioned response that is giving you in a false sense of safety? It is important to learn the distinction and recognize what is serving you. That awareness can actually save your life."

"It takes lifetimes of living in physical reality to learn, to discern, to choose, to become aware and live a marvelous loving life. That is YOUR gift to SELF and to all CREATION."

M–"Right! The *Flow* means being tuned into or moving with Love, wisdom, experience, and inner guidance. The alternative is fixated with the mind's limitations. Conditioned responses are not really serving the self as they are full of judgments and fears. On *Earth School,* as it has been called, there are endless opportunities to move beyond the challenges and suffering we may find in life. Again, it reminds me of the quote from Jesus, *'Knock and the door will be opened. Seek and ye shall find.'"*

K–"We are surrounded by this Love and Wisdom and it never ends. In or out of a body our Spirit continues on, always expanding with Love."

M–"So, what I know today, or in this moment, might change. We are always evolving, right? It's about just staying open?"

K–"That's it, Mom. *Just stay open.* Remember? Love you as big as the expanding Universe."

M–"Thank you for this time together again."

As I felt the deep peace and inner joy of our sharing, I looked out to the forest and everything for a few moments was still. It was very strange, as if the world stopped around me…not even a tweet from a bird. Ahhh, the comfort was beyond words, but deeply felt. After this surreal moment—a deep peace that felt like a hole in time—reality slowly returned. The sound of the wind gradually became louder through the treetops and the chipmunks began scampering around the boulders in front of my chair. This deep connection to Oneness was such a gift, "I feel expanded. Thank you, Kevin!"

LOVE NEVER DIES

July 17, 2019

IN PURE BEING

On the way down the mountain, as we left the family campground, I asked out loud, "Show us a wonderful campsite with babbling brook and waterfalls." Shortly after we passed the Ranger station, I heard, "Turn Left." We followed the guidance and discovered a hidden and deserted place down the road.

"God day! We have found a beautiful private campsite, right next to a sparkling stream. Thanks for the loving support that brought us to this place and you too Kevin."

"Kevin, I would like you to come and speak to me about the following… I was re-reading in the book "The Power of Now" by Eckhart Tolle, and a question emerged about your spiritual experience. Have you relinquished your attachment to the past and future so you could enter the '*Now*'? I was wondering if you experience pain or suffering from your past."

K–"Hey Mom. Glad you found the stream; just what you and Bryan needed."

M–"It is so perfect and beyond my wildest expectations. And no one else around! Thank You."

K–"Glad to help and glad *you asked.*"

M–"OK, the question…"

K–"I am certainly *NOT* in pain because *I am now in Pure Being, where* there is no suffering. There is, however, awareness of the past, of course, or how would I even remember who you are or who I thought I was as Kevin?"

M–"Of course. Who you *thought* you were as Kevin?"

K–"While you saw me as Love and Joy and knew I was capable of anything, I had forgotten the connection to my higher-self, or to Love. You knew I had Angels with me, and I would have been able to connect. Yet, I did not choose to reach out while I was there in my earth body. My mind was stuck trying to deal with the struggles in my life."

"I can only say, from this place of Love and *Pure Awareness,* that I now want to experience life differently. I don't know if I will get to come back, but I know Love is the key. I am learning to *be and feel* that Love within me."

"Awakening from our mental, emotional, or physical suffering on earth is a gift we are given… *TO WAKE UP* means choosing a new perspective and going beyond our conditioned ideas about what life appears to be. There are endless ways to find freedom and joy while living a physical life. While I could say that I am missing a lot, like being there with you with my toes in the cold running stream, I am here and there in observation with so many I love. I am not stuck in the past because there is so much more. Where you are is Heaven on Earth, *right now!* Where I am is Heaven and I can see and feel deeply. I might not be able to touch you with a body, but I can with my heart and the words you can hear."

M–"I will touch the stream, pet my sweet dog Kilo, and make love with my husband Bryan, because *I CAN. Life is good* and it is a gift. I feel even more blessed to be part of life, as my conversations with you remind me how precious it is. Thank you, Kevin."

K–"Thank you, Mom, for taking the time to listen and know that *OUR LOVE NEVER DIES!* Live it fully, Mom."

July 22, 2019

THE TRUTH OF HEARING

M–"It is a God Day, yes, another beautiful day here by a babbling creek in the High Sierras."

I felt touched by Christ and heard the following words:

"You open to feel my Heart presence. You know I am unconditional Love and your willingness to open and to let go is the key. Here, you sit in perfect harmony at the foot of the fresh mountain stream. Listen to the sounds of the water dancing over the rocks, look at the beauty of the large ferns, bright green and lush with life; this is my gift to you. Not just because you prayed aloud for the perfect and awesome campsite, but because I Love you and I want you to let go of all your concerns about Bryan's health. *He is in my hands.* Your focus is to Love yourself and Love your husband. You recognize the importance of your time with the Infinity Love Process, and your time of meditation to become still, listen and receive. Know that you are embraced by your Angels, and loved by me, Jesus the Christ, in more ways than you will ever know! Witness the visit of the hummingbird dancing across the stream and hovering for just a moment to say hello. I shall send small gifts of Love that you will notice."

"Give your worry and fear of the time that Bryan will come home to me. *Trust in Divine Timing for ALL concerned.* Be with the beauty of NOW. Now is all there is."

MY RESPONSE

M–"Thank you! Such a small thing to say but I am deeply humbled by your Love. I am moved to tears and yet the hummer danced near me again and my heart lightened. The sound of thunder awakens me to all the *power of your Love.* I am grateful beyond any words I can express.

God's beauty is all around me and your Love enfolds me. Between the words, I feel *a peace deeper* than any moment I can remember..."

"Oh! I do, however, remember when I was five years old. I felt my Angels around me when I was lost in the Black Forest, and I was almost eaten by the wild boar! Aww, I remember the *peace* that came over me, calming my fright and fear that I thought was the end of me. Aww, I felt the calm, the reassurance of the Angels that appeared and took me by the hand to lead me back home."

I was so deeply moved by this direct communication from Christ. There was no doubt about it, in my truth of hearing, I was so clear and *full of Love and deep reassurance*. I took out my pen and pencil and began to sketch the beauty that was before me...

"Come unto me, all ye that labor and are heavy laden, and I will give you rest."
—Jesus (Matthew 11:28)

Chapter 17

The Other Side

"Stay blind to any fears or limitations and open your eyes to the inexhaustible power and infinite possibilities already inside you."
—Hiral Nagda

It has been five years since Kevin's passing and my communications with him have continued. I realized there must be a stopping point to my sharing with you or I would never get this book out. I had to pick and choose which interactions to share and find a stopping point. New questions would always come to mind, and I believe that some readers may find some of his answers from the Spirit world interesting. So, I will share this heart-to-heart session as I asked him this question, "What is it like being on the other side?"

July 21, 2020

LAST COMMUNICATION?

Bryan and I decided that a road trip to our piece of heaven in Baja would be just what we needed, even though we had to be extra careful as the pandemic was still not under control. My times in nature by the water's edge always seemed to be the perfect place to connect with Kevin.

M–"God Day Christ, my Angels, Guides, and my Kevin in Heaven. Be with me now. Tell me Kevin, what can you tell me about being on the other side?"

M–"Hello Kevin, are you there?"

K–"Yes Momma, I am. Nice stream, glad you are on this journey."

M–"Me too, I needed a break."

K–"It's a good thing."

M–"So, what can you share with me about what goes on, on the other side?"

K–"It's not boring here. There is much going on but in a most peaceful way. Each Soul moves towards or is guided to the next level of expansion (internal expansion). There is an awareness of a new level, a stretching beyond to a greater sense of beingness."

M–"So, is it education of the Soul?"

K–"Yes, not experiential learning, the way it is done through the mind and body, but experiential expansion of the Spirit. It is a graduation from worrying about how things will unfold. Humans can tend to always weigh every aspect of self-expression that will be seen by others. Now, I fully enjoy choices in this reality with a freedom of expression that neither I, nor another being will judge. I am fully expressing ME."

M–"Is it an Earth-like environment? Like plants, etc.?"

K–"Imagine Heaven on Earth but even more beautiful and without pain or suffering. A place of limitless possibilities, with no money or time limitations. Of course, on Earth we limit ourselves through our thoughts and that limits our experience. The reality is that we have made up those perceived limitations, or blocks, which were never truly there. *There was always a way beyond.*"

"By being in Spirit and knowing expansiveness immediately, because of not having a physical body and not being held by dense energy, your awareness begins this evolution."

"After a phase of integration, you have a life review of your earthly experience and of your reactions. You observe if you had a closed or open heart with yourself and with everyone you have interacted with. Simply put, were you kind or unkind? Were you limiting your Love with yourself or with others? You reflect on what you learned or did not learn about compassion."

M–"And then what?"

K–"With assistance, by loving and supportive Energies, you see without judgment the level of awareness from which you had operated. With this full awareness, you then observe how your actions were either uplifting or were they hard on others. It is a phase of gathering **TRUE AWARENESS** of your Soul's journey to this point."

M–"And now?"

K–"Now, you can see and observe your past and your present. I have chosen to be a Guide with you, and I have continued to expand my awareness of *Love* and its many dimensions…without any of my old, preconceived limitations. I want to come back and learn to make a difference with *Love* and *authentic* Joy *for* all. I am still waiting and learning until this time comes."

M–"Do you think this may happen soon?"

K–"God's timing Mom. *God's timing.*"

M–"OK, Kev, I thank you for all your sharing in a way that I can hear. I may not fully get it, but I am understanding more and more each time."

LOVE NEVER DIES

"I Love you as Big as the Expanding Universe and Beyond! Forever and Always!"

K–*"Love You Too, Mom!"*

Chapter 18

Unconscious Decisions

"If a problem is fixable, if a situation is such that you can do something about it, then there is no need to worry. If it's not fixable, then there is no help in worrying. There is no benefit in worrying whatsoever."
—Dalai Lama XIV

My husband had made it through a major open-heart surgery and was finally given the green light from the doctors, to return to our "happy place" back in Baja Sur Mexico. That was our light at the end of the tunnel.

Bryan had many failed procedures and surgeries because of his unique heart, yet each operation revealed more information for his medical team. Finally, after waiting two years, he had a successful open-heart surgery. It was an amazing operation that his surgeon, Dr. Pitiorus of UCSD said, "This will go down in the medical journals!"

It has been three weeks since we arrived and are finally settled and slowing down to life on the beach once again. Watching the pelicans and osprey swooping over the aqua blues of the Sea of Cortez is a peaceful past time as we kick back in our much appreciated zero gravity chairs. It has been a very long year and we are so grateful to finally get back to this wonderful place.

April 21, 2021

GUILT

It has been a month to the day that my mother, Hope Rudh, has passed. She passed on at 98, dying of natural causes but had held on for years in pain with back and neck injuries and too many other complications to list. Growing old for her was not a peaceful process. She was cranky and angry. She would scream, "Help, help" and would bark orders to all! No one was amazed more than my brother by her tenacity to hang in there. He had come to live with her eight years earlier, having had a bad divorce, and now he was her main caretaker. Not at all an easy task.

After a few sessions watching Kevin and I communicate, she jumped right into the subject she knew much about, WORRY. I thought she might have something to say about this topic and I was writing as fast as I could with her willingness to share and listen.

M–"God Day Christ, my Angels, my guides, my Kevin, and Mom in Heaven. Please speak to me on the subject of worry, now that you are possibly seeing from a new perspective?"
Then I heard…

[Please note, in the following discussion, 'M–' is Janice's mom, Hope Rudh, and 'J–' is for Janice.]

M–"Jan?"

J–"Mom? Speak up!"

M–"I like your beach and all your paintings and creativity."

J–"Thanks Mom, so glad you can see from there, 'hoped' you would."

M–"I am quite amazed at all I can see by just wanting to connect with someone with Love."

J–"You have a lot of Love with you on your side too?"

M–"Yes, Mom and Dad and Herbert, your Dad are here. Kevin was there right away as I left my body and so many waiting. Peg, your Aunt Maxine and so many other family members and friends were all on the other side waiting in the Golden Light."

J–"The Light of Jesus?"

M–"Yes, God is so good."

J–"Yes Mom. I wish you could have experienced peace and beauty on this side."

M–"Me also, honey. I was just filled with too much worry. I WORRIED ABOUT EVERYTHING!"

J–"Yes, I saw that you did. It was hard to watch, and I was sad to see you couldn't let go and let God more in your life. Can you see why this was your way of thinking now?"

M–"The little girl inside me was still afraid."

J–"Can you tell me what made you so afraid?"

M–"We were living on the farm in Minnesota. Mom and Dad had been fighting and upset for days and then it went quiet."

J–"How old were you?"

M–"I was about six or seven. I heard my mother crying and calling out to my dad. I ran into the kitchen and there he was curled up under the table crying and looked so afraid. I crawled under the table, and I reached out my hand to reassure him it was safe to come out as my mother quieted down as well."

J–"I remember you mentioning that to me once. Hard to understand as a child to see your Daddy so afraid and upset?"

M–"So, I decided if I wasn't worried and concerned about them, I wasn't being a good girl. A good girl loves their mom and dad and should take care of them or something bad will happen to them. Then who will take care of my little sister and me?"

J–"Right, but that was a lot to take responsibility for a child and was it your job really?"

M–"No, but it seemed so to me."

J–"Can you see how you carried that intense sense of responsibility and worry forward in your life?"

M–"OH YES! If I wasn't worrying, then I wasn't being a good mother or grandmother or friend!"

J–"Or a 'good girl'?"

M–"Yes!"

J–"So, you think caring means you are supposed to really worry?"

M–"OH YES!"

J–"*Really*? How does that help?"

M–"Well, looking back I guess it really didn't help at all. It just was something I thought I was supposed to do."

J–"As you grew and studied about Jesus and God it seem to give you some comfort."

M–"Yes, the Lord is good and loves us more than we know."

J–"But when we pray and ask for help for yourself or another, aren't we then to *let go and let God* work it out? Right?"

M–"Yes, but I didn't believe that I could."

J–"Do you see how, at least from my perspective and for other family members, like my brother Gordon and your grandson Chad, that was a bit crazy making, especially the older you got? You became worried and anxious about every little thing. You were not at peace about anything. Can you see that now?"

M–"Yes, I really made a mess of things and see how I pushed people away."

J–"Well, it was hard to live with that deep anxiety especially for Gordon and hard for the rest of us to watch."

M–"I am so sorry Dear, I really am. I am sorry I was so difficult. I really carried my fear out to the end."

J–"Yes Mom, I was so deeply sorry to see you suffer and not find happiness."

M–"And I pushed you and Gordon and Chad and Arie away! I guess even Sable too?"

J–"I want you to know how much I love you and understand. I really do. I understand because of having worked with so many people through the years and the work I have done on myself. I understand how deeply the decisions we make from traumatic situation can be carried on into our life unconsciously. Nonetheless, it is motivating all our reactions in life in so many dysfunctional ways. It is often hidden in the subconscious until it comes up to really be seen in the light of love."

"I believe when one is safe and supported in Love you can finally see the truth that sets you free. I believe that *is* the Grace of God in action. I do not think we necessarily need to die to look back because that freedom is available in the here and now. Are you still with me Mom?"

M–"Yes my Dear it is true. I wish I knew that much earlier."

J–"Yes me too, I believe you would have been happier and had more ability to see and trust in the Good/God in life."

M–"I have No doubt."

J–"No time like the present Mom and it is never too late. I Love you Mom and I am so grateful for your being present with me. I am so happy for your Peace and understanding in this moment. I am looking forward in honoring you at your upcoming memorial in a couple weeks with all the family and friends that love you."

M–"Thank you my Dear, I am sure it will be lovely."

J–"Yes, be at Peace and know you will always be loved by me. I am happy you are my mother. Thank you."

M–"And, I am happy you are my daughter!"

J–"Thank you."

> *"Worry never robs tomorrow of its sorrow,*
> *it only saps today of its joy."*
> —Leo Buscaglia

WORRY: A CHRONIC DYSFUNCTION

I shared this conversation with my mom because worry really can become a chronic dysfunction of the mind. We can go into patterns of self-disturbing thoughts, and it is hard to find a way out when you do not have a clear understanding of what is really motivating this automatic response. Do not accept unhappiness as a norm. Find your freedom with self-understanding. Seek counsel. Stay open to learn another way to your freedom and happiness in the here and now. When you find your Oneness with all that is, you will find self-mastery.

While life might sometimes bring you to your knees, you have to trust and listen. I have recently been reminded of this message when watching the movie *LIFE ITSELF* (Written and Directed: by Dan Fogelman). It is one of the best stories about Love found and Love lost that I have seen in a long time. It brings hope to the broken-hearted.

Without revealing any spoilers, at one point in this movie, a dying mother asks her very devoted son to go off to university. She says, "You have done enough. Listen to me, Rigo. You had many ups and down in your life…too many. And you will have more. This is life and this is what it does. Life brings you lower than you think you can go. But if you stand back up…and go a little farther…you will always find Love." With tears flowing, she continues, "So you go now. Give me a beautiful life, the most beautiful life ever. Yes? And if life brings us to our knees… You stand us back up. You get up and go farther and find us the Love. Will you do that?"

Yes, life will surprise us. It brought me to my knees in an agony I thought I could not bear. I got back up. I went a little further and Kevin's Love surprised me. I know now, for sure, that Love Never Dies, not just for me but for all of us. Take a deep breath and just keep going. Love is always waiting.

*"The truth will set you free.
Being vulnerable is courage.
You are Love and Loved.
Love lives through each of us.
Let your Light shine bright!"*
—Janice Hope

Chapter 19

The Continuum of Love

"Out beyond wrong doing and right doing there is a field of luminous consciousness. I will meet you there"
—Rumi

I hope that our journey and heart-to-heart discussions have been helpful. Our intention was to help everyone remember who they are and realize they have so much Love and support around them.
There is a lot more that I could share but this last discussion sums up the essential.

June 15, 2022

GO BEYOND

M–"God Day, Christ, my Angels, Guides and my Kevin in Heaven."

"I ask you, Kevin, to come through and speak clearly to me about the last chapter. Is there something you would like me to say to people that will be uplifting and inspiring? Or is there anything you want to say to me? Are you here? Can you hear me?"

K–"I am. I was happy to see family and friends at Sable's graduation from UCLA. This is a great beginning of her life. She will go far in making a positive difference in the awareness of what needs to happen to save the planet. Love it or abuse it. That is the choice. She will do it her way to make it clear."

M–"Yes, I believe she can and will make a positive difference!"

K–"Yes, I guess that is the point. Making a positive difference. I feel I missed the chance in my lifetime. I believe I missed the opportunity."

M–"Well, maybe not. Seems like one can awaken from wherever they are in their life. It is more difficult, when you are in 'survival mode,' to ask questions such as, 'Am I making a positive difference?' 'How can I contribute to others or to the planet?' 'Am I taking action to do what I can?' or 'What brings me Joy?' But these are the important questions!"

K–"OK, right Mom, and it's never too late. The good news is, even from this side, I can make a difference, only if you ask."

M–"And I believe that is true Kevin, and you have proved that in many ways. I believe that is why I have persevered through the last almost seven years now to write about our connection. It is wonderful that I can hear you, as you have shared so much with me, but I don't think one necessarily has to hear to know and remember the important thing, that Love never dies! Loved ones are with us, even if they can't be heard. The connection we have to people we have loved continues on. We must believe and move through the feelings of loss and sadness to a place of gratitude. Being thankful for the gift of the connection, not only the one we had, but that we still have, opens the loving support from the other side. Thank you, Kevin, for our ongoing connection and for the Love that we share."

K–"OK, I love you. You have made this possible by your courage to connect."

M–"Hmmm! Strangely enough, it does take courage to step into the void and really let go of any needs. Letting go of my personal needs and the deep vulnerability of the hurt and pain of how you took your life

THE CONTINUUM OF LOVE

was very hard. I had to lay those aside, enough to go deeper, to really listen."

K–"OK, yes Mom. You could have gotten stuck there, but you didn't. You had the courage to feel and go beyond."

M–"Go beyond? Yes, to a happier and fulfilling life?

K–"That's your choice. Helping people and reminding them that they can also go beyond their pain of loss."

K–*"We are in a Continuum of Love!"*

    This was a powerful moment. I had to stop and really feel my heart expanding with that truth. It was like waves of Energy and Love expanding from my heart. It was huge and vibrant, full of color and light. It seemed to stretch all over the planet. As it expanded, I felt this huge influx of Love returning to me.
    I wished I could paint this experience, but it is moving. It is not stagnant and expands to all, from me and from Kevin. Love cannot be broken; it is whole. This beautiful living energy is a powerful vibration that never ends.
    Take a deep breath to feel how you are a part of this Oneness and expanding Love right now.
    Peace be with you.

Thankful (by Rebecca Jade)

I wanted to share an inspirational song from Rebecca Jade, the musical director at Seaside Center for Spiritual Living. These uplifting words, from this award-winning artist, resonated deeply for me. I would encourage you to listen to the song from her website (rebeccajade.com) while reading the lyrics.

Look at me, look at me... my heart is broken,
I'm tired from dragging all this pain around

Could it be, could it be... my feet are trembling,
On what I thought was solid ground

Nobody can hear my cry,
As I scream within my mind
I guess a broken heart is part of life
How do I go on from here?

Be thankful, for the chance to love
From the good, the bad, the ups and downs,
Take the time to see the beauty in it all

Look at me, look at me... I'm still standing,
Even after my heart took a fall

Could it be, could it be... we are stronger than we think we are,
Even in our darkest hour we stand tall

Hellos and goodbyes...
Life is made of pulls and pushes, like the tides
And though you'll never leave my mind
I'm moving on from here

I'm thankful, for the chance to love
Through the good, the bad, the ups and downs,
Take the time to see the beauty in it all

LOVE NEVER DIES

Hellos and goodbyes...
Life is made of pulls and pushes, like the tides
And though you'll never leave my mind
I'm moving on from here

<u>And although, my heart hurts,</u>
<u>And I wish, that things were different</u>
<u>I know this, is my path</u>
<u>My journey is, my own to have</u>

—Rebecca Jade

Suggested Resources

BOOKS

Atlas of the Heart: Mapping Meaningful Connection and the Language of Human Experience, by Brené Brown

Dying to Be Me: My Journey From Cancer, Near Death, To True Healing, by Anita Moorjani

Emotional Healing: Experience Balance and Self-Empowerment in an Age of Rapid Change!, by Verlaine Crawford

Ending the Battle Within: How to Create a Harmonious Life Working with Your Sub-Personalities, by Verlaine Crawford

Healing the Hurt Spirit: Daily Affirmations for People Who Have Lost a Loved One to Suicide, by Catherine Greenleaf

I am Light I am Bright, (A Spiritual Coloring Book) by Melanie Lococo (MelanieLococo.com)

Living From the Mountain Top: Be the Mystic You Were Born to Be, by Christian Sorensen

Living the Science of Mind, by Ernest Holmes

Many Lives, Many Masters: The True Story of a Prominent Psychiatrist, His Young Patient, and the Past-Life Therapy That Changed Both Their Lives, by Brian L. Weiss

Practicing the Presence, by Joel S. Goldsmith

Proof of Heaven: A Neurosurgeon's Journey Into the Afterlife, by Eben Alexander, MD.

Reaching to Heaven: A Spiritual Journey Through Life and Death, by James Van Praagh

SOS: A Guidebook to Survivors of Suicide, by Jeffrey Jackson (American Association of Suicidology)
sprc.org/resources-programs/sos-handbook-survivors-suicide
suicidology.org/wp-content/uploads/2019/07/SOS_handbook.pdf

The Celestine Prophecy, by James Redfield

The Heart of Transformation: And the Butterfly Effect, by Verlaine Crawford

The Mastery of Love: A Wisdom Book, by Don Miguel Ruiz

The Power of Love: Connecting to the Oneness, by James Van Praagh

The Power of Now: A Guide to Spiritual Enlightenment, by Eckart Tolle

The Untethered Soul: The Journey Beyond Yourself, by Michael A. Singer

Taking the Cape Off: How to Lead Through Mental Illness, Unimaginable Grief and Loss, by Patrick J. Kenny

This Thing Called You, by Ernest Holmes

SUGGESTED RESOURCES

What If This Is Heaven?: How Our Cultural Myths Prevent Us from Experiencing Heaven on Earth, by Anita Moorjani

Your Best Life Now: Seven Steps to Living at Your Full Potential, by Joel Olstein

Your Truth, Know it, Speak It, Live It: A Guide for People Seeking Authenticity in their Personal and Professional Lives, by Eileen R. Hannegan, M.S.

OTHER RESOURCES

Seaside Center for Spiritual Living
Seaside Center for Spiritual Living is a loving, supportive community inspiring all to experience their spiritual unfolding, healing & growth through the principles of the Science of Mind. This spiritual family gratefully celebrates the abundance of life & honors each individual's unity with God. Visit their site for more information about Reverend Christian Sørensen and the Seaside community.
seasidecenter.org

JKYog (Jagadguru Kripaluji Yog)
This is a non-profit charitable organization established for the physical, mental, and spiritual well-being of all humankind. Their leader is Swami Mukundananda. They disseminate authentic knowledge of Yoga for the body, mind, and soul. It serves the needy, promotes education for the rural youth and provides healthcare for the underprivileged.
jkyog.org

SUICIDE PREVENTION AND SUPPORT

988 Suicide & Crisis Lifeline
The 988 Suicide & Crisis Lifeline is a national network of local crisis centers that provides free and confidential emotional support to people in suicidal crisis or emotional distress 24 hours a day, 7 days a week in the United States. We're committed to improving crisis services and advancing suicide prevention by empowering individuals, advancing professional best practices, and building awareness.
988lifeline.org
Dial or text **988**

American Foundation for Suicide Prevention (AFSP)
The American Foundation for Suicide Prevention is a voluntary health organization based in New York City, with a public policy office based in Washington, D.C. The organization's stated mission is to "save lives and bring hope to those affected by suicide."
afsp.org

The National Action Alliance for Suicide Prevention
The National Action Alliance for Suicide Prevention is an American suicide prevention organization coordinating national efforts to advance the National Strategy for Suicide Prevention.
theactionalliance.org

National Alliance on Mental Illness. (NAMI)
The National Alliance on Mental Illness is a United States-based advocacy group originally founded as a grassroots group by family members of people diagnosed with mental illness.
nami.org

SUGGESTED RESOURCES

San Diego Behavioral Health Services (BHS)
This department provides mental health and substance use disorder services to over 111,000 San Diego County residents of all ages. Services are provided through 9 county-operated programs, over 300 contracts, and 800 individual fee-for-service providers.
sandiegocounty.gov/hhsa/programs/bhs

Health Care Agency Behavioral Health Services (Orange County)
Depression. Anxiety. Drug and alcohol misuse. Hopelessness. There are many conditions that can affect your ability to manage your everyday thoughts, emotions and actions, also known as your "behavioral health." And in Orange County, there's one place to start getting help for all of them: OC Links.
855-OC-Links (855-625-4657)
ochealthinfo.com/oclinks

Compassionate Friends
A peer support group formed by and for parents whose children have died, irrespective of the child's age at death and the cause of death, and is independent of any religious, philosophical or government body.
compassionatefriends.org/surviving-childs-suicide

About the Author

Janice Hope is an author, teacher, motivational speaker, and Intuitive Healing Facilitator known as the Angel Lady.

She has been helping clients with their wellbeing for the last 35 years using various modalities, including Breath Work, Reiki, Chakra Balancing, Past-Life Regression, and the Infinity Love Process.

Janice works with Angels and Guides to help identify her client's core issues or the blockages behind symptoms. She is also a medium and receives insights from her client's loved ones on the other side.

Her sessions allow people to understand why they might feel stuck and identify the root of some of their core issues. Those answers will help heal the heart and support the grieving process. This provides ease and upliftment, which allows clients to carry on their journey after a loss or a challenging situation.

The wisdom or spiritual insight received provides an Energetic Integration, helping people feel the love, comfort, peace, and connection which they are seeking. The main realization is that they are not alone and are deeply loved. This awareness will encourage them to pursue their dreams and enjoy a fulfilling and happy life.

Janice has worked most of her life from the sacred ceremonial grounds of Idyllwild, California, honoring the Native American ways of our ancestors. From her teepee, she guided many drumming circles with her Soul sisters to experience a deeper connection with Great Spirit and God.

She also works from her dream home, in Baja California Sur, where she feels a profound connection with nature. This idyllic setting provides a source of inspiration for her work as a mixed media visionary artist. She loves to use oils, acrylics, watercolor and blend them with organic material, such as seashells and other natural elements. Mermaids have become the focus of her most recent creations.

Janice also enjoys singing and writing songs with her husband Bryan, who plays the ukulele.

To learn more about working with Janice or to book her for a speaking engagement or for a private session, please visit her website: **JaniceHope.com**

Additional Materials & Resources

Access your Additional Materials & Resources referenced throughout this book at JaniceHope.com/lovebonus